humorous approaches. The stories, told in a vibrant and capti-
vating voice, ranging from thought provoking and insightful
to adventurous and hilarious, are a delightful read.   The
charming characters of broad cultural variety bring the whole
world into your hands, making hearts bond over a jolly good
laugh. And frankly, what can be better?'

Marit Imeland Gjesme, Founder of CultureCatch®
intercultural training consultancy

Praise for *Close Encounters of a Cultural Kind*

'A kaleidoscope of beautiful stories! I absolutely enjoyed this journey across different cultures especially being able to relate to some of them. I had a chance to live and work in Japan, so needless to say, I have a soft spot in my heart for that country. The Japanese salesman story is a great example of how different Western and Eastern cultures can be, especially when it comes to relationship building and communication. This book, full of real life stories and critical incidents, is an excellent guide that will give you the right set of tools to understand people from a reality that may be vastly different than yours, and will help you to develop what the world sometimes needs most of all – cross-cultural empathy.'

Marina Dzhashi, Moscow-based cross-cultural consultant
and host on "International Business Ethics"

'This book is a delicious smorgasbord of cross-cultural experiences and adventures, recounted in an amusing and easily digestible style. A delightful array of quirky encounters, unbelievable scrapes and the kindness of strangers, it is also testament to truth being stranger than fiction. From selling bikes in China for fistfuls of dirty banknotes, to speeding across the desert in Abu Dhabi in a brand new Mercedes and trying to buy a dining table in Japan, Richard learns something from every cross-cultural encounter and is not ashamed to admit that he didn't always get it right, despite facing new opportunities with enthusiasm and an open mind. His insights into North Korea were fascinating and his description of a Japanese-Brazilian training group had me laughing out loud. Buy it and enjoy!'

Patti McCarthy, author of *Cultural Chemistry: Simple Strategies for Bridging Cultural Gaps*

'"Lapland is the real land of Finland. It is a land where thoughts are unhurried, where words are few and where solitude is greatly valued. The tourist will enjoy this country if he can understand the silence." This quotation is characteristic of Richard Lewis´s new book. I love it, partly because of the author's surprising ending remarks in several of the chapters. He declares that the Greenlandic fishermen have a keen sense of humour, tolerance of other cultures and are rather easy-going. You could say the same about the writer of this book. Read, learn, smile and enjoy!'

Uno Grönkvist, former Senior Vice President Corporate Relations, Swedish Telecom

'*Close Encounters of a Cultural Kind* is another addition to Richard Lewis's fascinating library of analyses of cultures and cultural trends. This time, however, it's personal. Lewis relates his personal encounters as he travels around the world in stories rich in observation, insight and entertainment. With a preface by Milton Bennett, another noted cultural analyst, Lewis travels from Europe to the Far East, the Middle East and the Americas to bring us stories of people and places we hardly expect. For interculturalists in search of case studies and the general reader alike, it's a fascinating and thoroughly enjoyable read.'

Barry Tomalin, author of *World Business Culture: a Handbook*

'Historically, "cultural encounters" have often created wars and split people. In this precious little gem of a book, Richard shows how beautifully cultural barriers can be overcome when people meet face-to-face. How we, despite different outlooks, can build bridges across cultural gaps with mindful, respectful and

Close Encounters of the Cultural Kind, a painting
by Richard D. Lewis

CLOSE ENCOUNTERS OF A CULTURAL KIND

OTHER BOOKS BY RICHARD D. LEWIS

The Ballinger's
Cross-cultural Communication: A Visual Approach
The Cultural Imperative
Finland, Cultural Lone Wolf
Fish Can't See Water
Humour across Frontiers
Memoirs of a Linguist: The Road from Wigan Pier
Robert Lewis and His Son Jake
When Cultures Collide
When Teams Collide

CLOSE ENCOUNTERS OF A CULTURAL KIND

Lessons for business, negotiation and friendship

RICHARD D. LEWIS

NICHOLAS BREALEY
PUBLISHING
London • Boston

First published by Nicholas Brealey Publishing in 2020

An imprint of John Murray Press
A division of Hodder & Stoughton Ltd,
An Hachette UK company

1

A CIP catalogue record for this title is available from the British Library

Trade Paperback ISBN 9781529308136
eBook ISBN 9781529308143

Typeset in Celeste & Zurich BT by Palimpsest Book Production Ltd, Falkirk, Stirlingshire
Printed and bound in Great Britain by Clays Ltd, Elcograf S.p.A.

John Murray Press policy is to use papers that are natural, renewable and recyclable products
and made from wood grown in sustainable forests. The logging and manufacturing processes
are expected to conform to the environmental regulations of the country of origin.

John Murray Press
Carmelite House
50 Victoria Embankment
London EC4Y 0DZ

Nicholas Brealey Publishing
Hachette Book Group
Market Place Center, 53 State Street
Boston, MA 02109, USA

www.nicholasbrealey.com

In memory of Peter Sykes

CONTENTS

PREFACE

Richard Lewis is definitely old-school intercultural. I say this with fondness and a real respect for the 'second generation' – professionals who blazed trails that opened the new field for further exploration. Richard began his international adventures immediately in the wake of the publication of E.T. Hall's seminal *Silent Language*, the first book that mentions 'intercultural communication'. Richard subsequently made his own substantial contribution to the framing of cultural differences, but this book is something different. It is more about his direct experience of cultural differences than it is about explanations of them, told in a voice which is direct and not filtered by academic jargon

The first story, 'Bangor', presents Richard's style admirably. After setting the context with recognizable details of an innovative language program, he provides a few broad-brush descriptions of cultural behavior: 'The Italian men danced with the blonde Finnish girls. . . The Finnish men occupied the bar. . . The Japanese stood around modestly. . .'. He never actually says that Italians are like this and Finns are like that. He simply presents his observations of the behavior without omitting the cultural affiliations. I suppose a naïve reader might think he was stereotyping the cultures, but his statements are seldom about cultures *per se*; rather, they are about people who happen to be from certain cultures. I think the appropriate reading of these statements is to take them as details in a story, not as claims made about groups of people.

Although it is clearly not Richard's goal in this book to convey conceptual framing of his stories, I nevertheless think it would be useful to offer a definition of cultural generalizations and how they differ from cultural stereotypes. Anytime we talk about anything, we are generalizing (categorizing) to some extent, since otherwise we would only be able to describe our sensory sensations. The moment we categorize our perception as 'a cow', we have generalized, since, as semanticists have long taught, cow1 is not cow2. Similarly, person1 is not person2, but it is useful to intercultural communication to define certain forms of behavior that are more or less common to particular groups of persons and that differ across groups.

Generalizations about culture are not so much about the culture than they are about the observational categories that are used to distinguish the cultural behavior. One of the original examples of this kind of category is E.T. Hall's distinction of *low context* and *high-context* communication behavior. Hall did not intend to characterize entire cultures as more low or high context; rather he claimed that the distinction *might* be useful in identifying a potential cultural difference in communication behavior that could impact cross-cultural understanding. Richard Lewis followed that tradition in formulating his categories of linear-active, cyclic, etc.

Cultural generalizations become stereotypes when they are rigidly applied, particularly when the claim is made that a generalization applies to every individual in a group. For instance, it is a true generalization that you are more likely to find linear-active style represented in European American and

Northern European cultures. But it becomes a stereotype if you assume that a particular American or European uses that style. In other words, generalizations are statements of probability, not descriptions of actuality. This explains why you shouldn't make a cultural generalization from having met one or a few people from a cultural group. It is a stereotype to assume that particular individuals are 'representative' of the group!

Now, returning to the first story, Richard is saying something about specific Italians. It is really up to us to decide if this particular behavior fits accurate cultural generalizations about the group. I live part-time in Northern Italy, teach in an Italian university, and read a lot about Italian culture. I know a few Italian men who might not find blonde Finnish women attractive, but I'd say that by describing the Italian men in this way, Richard is implying an accurate generalization about young Italian men's interest in women over their interest in drinking. From my quasi-Italian perspective, I was particularly amused by Richard's description of the Italian men unapologetically switching from macho challenges to realistic self-preservation at the end of the story. It seems to be a good example of the generalization that Italians are concerned with image, but not to the point of stupidity!

In addition to Europeans, Richard gives a lot of attention to East Asian cultures, particularly Japan and Korea. I have less experience in South Korea and none in North Korea, but I found Richard's observations about the time he spent there compelling and relevant to our current understanding of those countries. With his keen eye for detail and his ear for dialogue, Richard gives us the view that a thoughtful non-specialist might have of those places. For those of us who in fact are specialists in intercultural communication, it is refreshing to read these relatively non-analytical descriptions. Of course, Richard is capable of being analytical, but he mostly restrains himself to give us this more layperson's view. He does show his analytic side in the story 'Back to the Future', which is introduced by an interesting treatise on Richard's linear-active/cyclic time distinction, but then moves on to one of the innumerable 'time is flexible' situations that most of us have experienced.

I was particularly struck by the subtle insights offered in Richard's stories about Japan. Having considerable professional experience there, many of his observations rang true to me. For instance, in the story about obligation ('The Akakura Skier'), he describes a behavior that many of us who have worked in Japan have noticed (probably less dramatically). The story includes a description of an injured skier who first avoids and then accepts obligation to his helpers, and a father whose child was saved and who miserably could not repay the debt. He raises the same theme in the story ('Fire in Shoto-cho') about a rich man whose house burnt and who was thereby indebted to the neighbors for their inconvenience. The English language demands 'repay the debt' in this situation, but that phrase does not really capture the idea that the relationship is *out of balance*. It is impossible to be 'out of debt' in this kind of situation – one can only accept the special obligation that has been incurred by the circumstance.

As a generalization, obligation in Japan is not just a temporary inequity in otherwise egalitarian conditions. Rather, obligation pervades all relationships, both those that involve hierarchical differences and those among "equals." Rather than attempting to avoid or eliminate obligation, as is the wont of many Northern Europeans and European Americans, people in Japan are more likely to engage in reciprocal gifting or favoring that is carefully balanced to move tolerable levels of obligation back and forth among the related people. A traumatic event can upset the balance irretrievably, as Richard alludes to with his stories.

But it doesn't take a traumatic event to upset the balance of obligation a little, as illustrated by a recent cultural faux pas I apparently made with a former student in Japan. She had invited me to speak at a conference and spent prodigious amounts of time arranging for my visit. Without much consideration other than European American gratitude (I'm embarrassed to admit), I presented several gifts to her and her husband. I was surprised and then chagrined when, just before I departed, I was presented with twice as many gifts as I had given. Upon reflection and confirming it to be the case, what had happened was that I had not correctly factored in the lifelong obligation incurred by a student to his or her teacher, and my excessive gifts had tipped the relationship a little out of balance. In discussing the situation, my student points out that *giri* is an obligation that can be repaid, but *on* is one that cannot be repaid – only carefully balanced.

It is not accidental that most of the first and second-generation interculturalists and many of the rest of us – I am probably the 2.5-generation – spent a lot of time in Japan. One of the first uses of observational categories to describe cultural difference was Ruth Benedict's 1946 book *The Chrysanthemum and the Sword,* which was about Japanese culture. The first conference of interculturalists occurred in Japan, at International Christian University, 1972. And, as Richard notes, Japan presents Westerners with a lot of cultural surprises. But as he also demonstrates with his stories set in an array of national cultures, one can be surprised anywhere – including in one's own society.

Current applications of intercultural communication are

expanding the observation of relevant cultural differences beyond those of national societies. In fact, several of the original formulations of these techniques were made by contrasting different kinds of cultural groups – notably, Native American tribal groups. But it is true that many of the first two genera-tions of interculturalists focused on national cultural differences to exemplify the observations. There probably were several reasons for this, including the interest in (and funding for) understanding national cultural motivations in World War II, and the expansion of international travel and study abroad after that war. Today (2020), important cultural differences are no longer 'far away'. As Marshall McLuhan said so long ago (1964) in correctly predicting the multicultural future: 'In the *global village*, our neighbors will be profoundly different than us.' I believe he meant that in his future, we would not need to travel to be in contact with cultural differences – it would come to us. We are now living in that future. It has come to us through hyper-connected communication, immigration, political and climate refugees, more recognition of long-existing domestic cultural differences in ethnicity, gender, sexual orientation, and emerging cultures of identification. The frontier of intercultural communication is now next door.

Making intercultural communication relevant to successful living in multicultural societies is a two-pronged effort. One prong is to retrieve and reemphasize the roots of the field. That means going back to the origin of cultural relativity in recog-nizing the integrity of every worldview, not just those of national cultures. And it means recognizing how intercultural commu-nication bridged the separateness of unique worldviews by creating categories for observing and adapting to cultural differ-ences. The other prong is to develop new domestic strategies for bridging cultural differences without imposing one culture onto another – to develop the capability of mutual adaptation rather than one-way assimilation.

Assimilation has traditionally worked in two ways. One was the willingness of visitors and immigrants to 'do in Rome as the Romans'. The other was the insistence of host culture members that newcomers become as similar as possible to them. Both of these aspects of assimilation are now under revision. On the one hand, immigrants and particularly refugees are resisting the loss of their cultures entailed by assimilation. What used to be the 'third-generation' effect of immigrants' children assimilating and *their* children searching for their ethnic roots, has now shifted back to the immigrants themselves, or at least to their children, all insisting on maintaining ethnic heritage. Partially as a result of this commitment to multiculturality, the idea of 'when in Rome. . .' is changing to 'everywhere is Rome'. Once-dominant ethnic groups are losing their power to impose assimilation, and in response they are turning inward, seeking dominance through threatening others rather than incorporating them.

Assimilation is no longer sustainable, but the alternative need not be ethnic isolation and violence. Framing Richard Lewis' stories in the context of today's multicultural demands, we can see that he is evidencing an early form of mutual adaptation. Most of the people he describes are trying to get along with him, and he certainly is trying to get along with them. This is the model that we need to apply domestically – respect for each other's cultural differences, and a mutual willingness to go beyond tolerance and really engage one another in the business of building multicultural societies.

Milton J. Bennett, Ph.D.

Dec. 18, 2019

(1)

BANGOR, NORTH WALES

In the days when we used St Mary's College, Bangor, in North Wales, for English Language summer courses, we organized a different nationality mix every year. After a few years we decided some mixes were better than others and began to experiment in our recruiting. Spaniards, Italians and Portuguese were a bad mix as, at mealtimes, they tended to speak a mix of Romance languages that I thought of as 'neo-Latin' instead of practising their English. Greeks and Turks, Iranians and Iraqis, were a bad mix for other reasons.

One year we decided to recruit in just three countries, speaking languages so different that they would be obliged to communicate socially in English, and which were so far apart geographically that there would be no 'bad neighbour' problems. The recruiting grounds we chose were Finland, Italy and Japan. It was a compact three-week middle-level English course consisting of 50 keen students, mostly young businesspeople in their thirties. There were 20 Finns, 20 Italians and 10 Japanese. It was a nice triangle as each national group showed great interest in the 'exotic' nature of the two other countries. They garbled away eagerly (in English) during the opening cocktail. We congratulated ourselves.

The lessons went smoothly. We divided the students into five mixed-nationality groups of 10, depending on language levels. They all became good chums. The language units ran from 9am to 5pm with a one-and-a-half-hour lunch break and an evening social programme. We had wine-tasting evenings, conjurors, Scottish dancing, bellringing and singing competitions. Every Tuesday night we had a dance after dinner, and on Wednesdays we organized a full-day excursion to a place of historical interest (Welsh castles, Chester, Liverpool, etc.).

On the second Wednesday we planned to climb Mount Snowdon, Britain's second highest peak, which was situated only a few miles from the college. Though of impressive altitude, Snowdon is not a difficult mountain to climb. You can bus people halfway up it, and the rest is an invigorating four-hour slog to the summit, where a magnificent panorama of North Wales, the Mersey, Anglesey and half of Lancashire is on offer. All the students were enthusiastic about this particular excursion in the extreme. It made a welcome physical break from sitting six to seven hours a day in the classroom. The departure by bus was booked for 8.30 on the Wednesday morning.

On the Tuesday evening we had our usual dance after dinner. The pattern was familiar. The Italian men danced with the blonde Finnish women, the Finnish males occupied the bar (they would dance with the Italian women later) and the 10 Japanese stood modestly at one end of the dance floor watching everybody's feet to learn the steps. Everyone was having a good time.

Around 8pm it began to rain and by 8.30 it could be described as a downpour. Huge raindrops spattered on the windowpanes and rivulets could be seen flowing down the steep slope outside the college front door. At nine o'clock it was still raining cats and dogs. At this point three of the Finnish men uncharacteristically deserted the bar and came over to talk to me. They were Lehtonen, Lahtinen and Virtanen, three of the more advanced students.

'Mr Lewis.'

'Yes, gentlemen.'

'It is raining.'

'It is.'

'It is raining hard.'

'Very hard,' added Lahtinen.

'The rain will make Snowdon very – how do you say – muddy, tomorrow,' said Lehtonen.

I agreed with them.

'Mr Lewis, lets cancel the excursion,' suggested Virtanen.

I had to agree this was a sensible course of action. I had climbed Snowdon before on a wet day and knew it was a most unrewarding exercise. I went to the microphone and signalled to the band to stop playing.

'Ladies and gentlemen, I have an announcement. In view of the inclement weather, we have decided to cancel tomorrow's excursion.' Howls of dismay erupted from all the Italian men.

'What do you mean, cancel the excursion? It is the highlight of the week! It's included in our fee. Whose idea was this?'

Rather cowardly, I said: 'Well, the Finns thought . . .'

'The Finns are supposed to be tough men!' shouted another Italian.

The three Finnish males scowled.

'What kind of tough men are these, when they are afraid to go out if a drop of water falls from the sky?'

The Italians continued to jeer at the unfortunate trio.

I wanted to tell them that Finnish men are not very fond of being laughed at or made fun of in public, particularly by Italian men. I could see an ugly situation developing. Then I had what I thought was a brilliant idea.

'Let's ask the Japanese,' I said.

Fifty-year-old Yamamoto-san, the leader of the youngish Japanese group, stared at me, aghast, from the back of the dance floor.

'Mr Yamamoto, what do the Japanese think about this?'

'What do we think?' repeated Mr Yamamoto mechanically. All the Japanese heads switched back and forth.

'*Choto matte kudasai*' (just a moment), said Yamamoto. The group of 10 retired to a huddle in the corner and conversed animatedly in Japanese for five minutes. Yamamoto returned to face me.

'Lewis-san. The Japanese delegation has made a decision. If the Italians win the day, we will be happy to go up the mountain with the Italians. If, on the other hand, the Finns win the day, the Japanese group will be happy to stay in and study with the Finns.'

I could have kicked him out of the college.

'Thank you, Mr Yamamoto, you have been most helpful.'

The Italian jeering continued and finally the Finns had no option.

'*No, sitten lähdetään* – all right, we'll go,' snapped Lehtonen. The unhappy trio went back to the bar and the Italians continued their dance. The Finnish men went to bed early.

It rained all night and I slept badly. At eight I got up, made coffee in my room, packed a couple of sandwiches, put on my old clothes and took my mac. I heard the bus arrive at the front door where it waited with engine idling. At 8.31 precisely I went down and jumped a couple of puddles to board the bus. The driver, disconsolate, greeted me wearily:

'Good morning, Mr Lewis.'

'Good morning, driver.'

I turned to greet the students. On the bus were 20 scowling Finns, 10 smiling Japanese. No Italians.

We had a bad day. Slogging up the mountain in the mud and slush, we reached the summit, soaked to the skin, around one o'clock. It was foggy. Visibility was down to about 50 yards. At a height of 3000 feet, one felt this was a waste of altitude. Of course, the Japanese took pictures – of Finns, me and themselves. The Finns drank coffee from flasks and proposed an early descent. Sliding down mud is almost worse than going up it.

We arrived back at the college – in appearance a bunch of 31 tramps – about 4pm, when we saw the Italians, in miraculously sudden sunshine, taking tea on the terrace with chocolate biscuits (a Finnish favourite). As we passed them, Lehtonen snarled to the Italian ringleader:

'Why didn't you come with us up the mountain?'

'We would have, but when we woke up it was raining,' replied the Italian without batting an eyelid.

2

THE JAPANESE SALESMAN

Simpson was a 'hotshot' salesman who worked for AIG (American Insurance Group). His colleagues often used the term 'hotshot' to describe him, as his sales technique was characterized by enthusiasm, spontaneity and sporadic impetuosity tempered by his undoubted charisma. He did not beat about the bush; he unapologetically charmed his would-be clients and was generally successful in rapidly closing the sale. He was so successful that AIG transferred him to Tokyo where there was a lot of potential business among quickly expanding Japanese companies.

During his first six weeks in Tokyo, Simpson did not close a single sale. His American supervisor concluded that his charismatic style – so successful in New York and Los Angeles – was ineffective when dealing with calm, reserved Japanese insurance managers. He resolved to give Simpson a month's training (which he should have had in the first place) to allow him to become acculturated to the Japanese mentality. He therefore assigned him to Ichiro Harada, AIG's top Japanese salesman, who took Simpson with him as he made sales calls. Language was no problem as Harada spoke excellent English and interpreters were always available when required.

One morning, with a humbled Simpson in tow, Harada went for his appointment with Akio Watanabe, the CEO of a sizeable

Japanese domestic appliance manufacturer that was doing very well exporting their products to a dozen foreign countries, including the United States.

It was not a cold call. AIG had secured the account three years earlier but knew that some Japanese insurance companies were after the business and sensibly visited Mr Watanabe regularly to maintain good relations. Ichiro Harada, as AIG's star sales executive, had been given the responsibility of safeguarding the account. Simpson was eager to see how he did it.

Watanabe greeted Harada rather affably and seemed pleasantly disposed towards Simpson, who had been introduced as a trainee. Watanabe and Simpson exchanged visiting cards in the Japanese manner, and everyone took a seat. Watanabe offered green tea all round and he and Harada began to chat in Japanese. Their tone was very courteous as usual, also visibly relaxed. Simpson, who had taken a six-week Japanese course before coming to Tokyo, was able to follow the gist of the conversation, though understanding very little. What he was able to perceive, however, was that the two men were not talking about insurance. He gleaned certain references to baseball, a festival in Kyoto and, of course, golf. The weather was also mentioned, but as the conversation progressed, over a period of almost half an hour, Simpson's understanding decreased as the two Japanese seemed to speak more rapidly, possibly more idiomatically. Certainly, they appeared more and more jovial.

Just when Simpson was beginning to wonder when Harada would get down to business (or at least mention insurance) Watanabe stood up, put his hand in the drawer of his desk and handed Harada a set of keys. Simpson knew the rule about meetings being concluded in Japan by the host getting to his feet, so he dutifully followed Harada out of the office of the

CEO, who gave both Harada and himself a cheery goodbye for now.

Harada took the bewildered Simpson into a nearby coffee shop to give the American an immediate post-mortem on the sales call. Simpson's questions were both to the point: why had Harada not even mentioned the account and why had Watanabe given him a set of keys?

Harada smiled indulgently as he explained, 'There was no need to mention business, as the account remains secure, as long as I say nothing that displeases President Watanabe. As he likes baseball and is a keen golfer, these subjects, as well as some others, are safe ground for discussion. I support the same baseball team and my golf handicap is inferior to his. I never talk about anything that might be controversial. A half hour's chat like this one, once a month, gives him occasions for relaxation. Normally he has to work 10 to 12-hour days and he welcomes this type of break. He cannot be bothered by strangers coming into his office trying to sell him insurance'.

'But what were the keys?'

'They are his car keys.'

'What will you do with them?'

'I will take his wife shopping.'

Simpson gaped. 'Shopping?'

'Yes, to the Takashimaya Department Store, which has some dresses she is interested in.'

'And when will you do this?'

'In half an hour's time when I go to his house. I am sorry I have to leave you this morning, but I hope you can find your way back to the office.'

'Yes, but can you explain a little more?'

This was the 1970s, when Japanese wives, as you probably

know, tended to stay home during the day. Harada smiled patiently. 'Mr Watanabe is a rich man. He has a lovely wife, two fine children, a big house, a luxury car and, of course, a good job. One thing he has not got is time. Mrs Watanabe does not like to make a one-hour journey on the Underground alone. She does not drive. Mr Watanabe drives into work – I shall pick up his car in the company garage in a few minutes. Of course, he could take his wife shopping on Sundays, but the department stores are hopelessly overcrowded at weekends and shopping can be exhausting and unpleasant. The best time to go shopping is on the morning of a weekday, that is NOW.'

'And you will drive her?'

'Of course. And at three or four in the afternoon I will drive her back home and then return the car, with keys, to Mr Watanabe's garage between five and six.'

'A full day's work.'

'That is correct.'

'But no mention of business.'

'It's the last thing he wants to talk about.'

Simpson swallowed hard. But he was not quite satisfied with what he had learned.

'Mr Harada, I see that your argument is foolproof. But one more thing: how did you get the account in the first place?'

Harada smiled again. 'That is another story.'

He told Simpson the following:

'I happen to live a quarter of a mile away from Mr Watanabe's house. He drives to work every day leaving his home at 7.30am. He always takes the same route, which means that he passes a bus stop very near where we both live. The bus concerned takes me to Ohte-machi (central Tokyo) and stops near my office. I made it my business to stand at this bus stop every morning at

7.25. Every day Mr Watanabe drove past me at a distance of 5 metres. Of course, he did not know me, but when he had passed me 20–30 mornings, he became aware of my presence. You could say that after two to three months I became a familiar figure. Whenever he looked at me en passant, I would smile at him and bow slightly. This is not unusual in Japan when we see a stranger regularly. We are very polite people and actually quite sociable inside, though foreigners are not always aware of this.

'In summer months, especially June and July, it can rain very heavily in Tokyo. You can get very wet queueing for a bus. In a particularly wet period in June about three years ago, Mr Watanabe drove past me as usual on his way to work. Some mornings I deliberately "forgot" my umbrella, and he would have noticed that I was soaked to the skin. I must have presented a pathetic figure with my drenched raincoat and humble brief-case. I never failed to nod to Mr Watanabe as he passed. One morning, in a real downpour, his car pulled into the bus stop and he picked me up.

'Of course, we chatted on the one-hour drive into town. He informed me about his business, and I told him about my lowly position as an insurance agent. The next morning, he picked me up again in another downpour. The third morning it was dry, but he picked me up anyway. After that he gave me a lift every day, though I purposely used another bus stop now and again. I did not wish to overdo things. Over time, we got to know each other quite well. We compared hobbies and part-time pursuits. He told me about his wife's problems with shopping. Of course, I humbly offered to help. We never discussed insurance, until one day he said he would like AIG to put in a quote. The rest, as you can see, is history.'

'But, Mr Harada, you must admit you were fortunate in that

Mr Watanabe was soft-hearted enough to pick you up in the rain.'

Harada shrugged. 'Not really. It was only natural. I would have done the same for him.'

3

NAPOLEON'S CHANDELIER

Sailing from Menton to Corsica usually takes about 12–14 hours in favourable conditions. We left in a 39-foot Moody yacht at 8am and expected to reach Ajaccio around 10pm. A black speck on the horizon at about two o'clock mushroomed rapidly in the following half hour and before 3pm we were in the middle of a Mediterranean summer storm with 40-knot gale force winds and 10-metre waves between which the Moody bobbed up and down like a fisherman's float in near-blackness. The tempest lasted 12 hours; we limped gratefully into the smallish Ajaccio marina at three in the morning, where we moored alongside the port side quay, which boasted a café, a bank, a ship's chandler's and a clothes shop. We tied up rapidly and, exhausted as we were, went to bed at quarter past three.

The quayside explosion occurred at 3.30 precisely, deafeningly close. The Moody leapt violently up, then down and sideways on its mooring ropes; the anchor nevertheless held firm. We tumbled out of bed, scrambled dizzily up the quivering stairs onto the deck and took in the scene. The café had had its windows blown out, dozens of menacing shards of glass littered the quay; the ship's chandler's had also lost its glass front and most of its wares had been blasted off the shelves and lay in piles on the floor; the clothes shop was untouched; the bank (between the café and the chandler's) had disappeared.

Pieces of furniture floated as far as 30 metres out in the marina, about a yacht's length from the Moody. We suffered no damage; a light assortment of debris adorned our foredeck.

The police screamed into the marina in three Renaults 20 minutes later. A fire engine soon followed, though there were few flames to extinguish. The bomb had not been of the incendiary variety, yet it had achieved its objective with admirable thoroughness. Even the bank's name had vanished – we learned later that it was the Société Générale.

The police and firemen did not hang around long. They seemed to be considerably less traumatized than we were. After half an hour's note-taking and a brief exchange of views with the firemen, the police drove off siren-less back to their stations – or their beds. The firemen, after a few more minutes' desultory watering of what was left of the bank's floorboards, followed suit. Two dozen yachtsmen had joined us and shared our deck, as we were nearest to the vanished bank. Neither the police nor the fire brigade bothered to ask us any questions or take any statements. A Swedish yachtie told us it was probably the work of the Union Corse – an independence-for-Corsica organization. Similar explosions were apparently regular occurrences. No big deal.

We slept without further disturbance to our night's rest – though I would not say very soundly – until 11, when we put together an English breakfast and made our touring plans. In view of Napoleon Bonaparte's Corsican origins, we decided that a visit to Napoleon's Ajaccio house – now a museum – was the most appropriate. We signed up for a guided tour at one o'clock and made our way up a quiet street leading to our destination. I must confess that I was not a little excited – certainly expectant

– as I had conceived quite an admiration for the dynamic French emperor, in spite of his enmity towards the English. About 20 people had assembled for the tour of the house. A young woman of around 25 was our guide. The tickets were surprisingly cheap.

Used as I was to Parisian splendour in many museums in the French capital, I was quickly disappointed by the trivial, mundane nature of the exhibits on offer at Napoleon's Ajaccio dwelling. Dusty glass cases sheltered unexciting pairs of socks, matchboxes, snuffboxes, handkerchiefs, barely legible, faded postcards, pens and pencils, two tattered coats, half a dozen cheap chairs, a low coffee table, a wooden stool, a rocking chair, a pair of leather gloves, battered gold cuff-links, half a dozen unidentifiable brooches, a discoloured pair of boots, several cracked cups – either plain or with unrecognizable motifs – a possible gravy bowl, a dozen dusty tumblers and two faded prints of horses that Napoleon would never have been seen dead on. The whole exhibition would have been a poor match for a Portuguese Saturday-morning flea market. The tourists and yachties accompanying us seemed to share our boredom and disappointment. We thought the Emperor deserved something palpably better in his country of origin.

The museum, however, had one redeeming feature – a brilliant, scintillating item that was completely ignored by our guide. The largish house had around 10 rooms, most of them medium size and uniformly undistinguished. One large central room, however, was exceptional. About 20 by 10 metres, it was described by the young guide as an occasional, modest ballroom. One could imagine 20 couples waltzing around the floor in relative comfort. The only furniture consisted of two dozen small wooden chairs lining the walls.

Dominating this otherwise unremarkable room, hanging

from a central point in the ceiling, was the most beautiful and perhaps the largest chandelier that I have ever seen. Consisting of many hundreds of pieces of exquisitely cut glass, it could have graced such imposing British cathedrals as Winchester or Durham; in fact, I am not aware of any church, palace or ducal abode in France itself that boasts any work of art as splendif- erous as the wonderful creation hanging in Napoleon's Ajaccio ballroom. Not that I was surprised that such a magnificent piece should belong to or be associated with the great emperor. On the contrary, I thought it was a shining tribute to his own fame, exploits and place in history. Surely a fitting, final, triumphant commemoration of Bonaparte's decades-long mastery of European political and military existence. But why had the young guide not even mentioned it? Why had she completely ignored it in favour of the snuff boxes and old boots?

I was not going to let her get away with it. As she ushered the visitors towards the exit, I cornered her near the door. She was Corsican, speaking slightly accented French and the broken survival English she needed for American, Asian and some European tourists.

'Mademoiselle.'

'*Oui, monsieur.*'

'The chandelier.'

'*Oui, monsieur.*'

'It's magnificent.'

She remained silent.

'There's nothing else in the museum that can compare with it.'

'*Je ne comprends pas, monsieur.*'

'Why did you ignore it? Don't you think the visitors would have been interested in it?'

'*Je ne sais pas, monsieur.*'

'Where was it made?'

'I don't know, monsieur.'

'It looks Czech to me. I've seen some smaller ones like it in Prague'

She held her tongue.

'Is there anywhere I can get more information about this chandelier?'

'I don't know, monsieur.'

'It is not mentioned in the museum's brochure?'

'*Non, monsieur.*'

'Don't you think that is rather strange?'

'*Je ne sais pas, monsieur.*'

I was not getting anywhere. I asked a few more questions – they only served to increase her nervousness. Looking at her wristwatch, she edged us towards the exit. When we were all outside, she locked the door and walked briskly away in the opposite direction we took.

Five years later, I shared a coffee with a famous Czech table tennis champion, Ladislav Moudrý, a close friend of mine. He was a well-travelled man, and I happened to tell him about our sailing in Corsica. When I mentioned the chandelier, he showed great interest and when I had finished, he chuckled quietly.

'Let me tell you something.'

'Yes, Ladislav.'

'Have you ever been to a World Exposition?'

'Several.'

'You have seen what they put in the pavilions?'

'Folkloric items, inventions, works of art . . .'

'Exactly. What do the Czechs excel at?'

'Beer and cut glass.'

'Exactly. In the Montreal Exposition in 1976, the Czechs served Pilsner Urquelle to everyone who entered the Czech Pavilion. What was the chief attraction?'

'Don't tell me . . . the chand—'

'The most beautiful and elaborate Czech chandelier of modern times. It was one of the highlights (some say the high-light) of the whole World Fair'

'I am not surprised. But . . .'

'Do you know what happens to the exhibits displayed in a World Exposition?'

'I suppose they are repatriated.'

'Right. They are packed up in a special container – very fragile you know – and sent off with the other Czech items to Prague by ship via Marseille.'

'And?'

'It never got there.'

'What did the architect say?'

'He said he put it on board – personally.'

'Are you saying that this chandelier is the same one I saw in Ajaccio?'

'You tell me. Did it look Czech?'

'Unmistakably.'

'Rather grand, was it?'

'I've never seen anything half so magnificent. But what did the Czech authorities say when it didn't turn up?'

'The Ministry of Culture was devastated.'

'And the architect?'

'He stuck to his story.'

'It must have been a very valuable work of art.'

'Priceless.'

Ladislav treated me to another of those muted, sardonic Czech chuckles.

I asked him, 'Have you heard of the Union Corse?'

'One of those independence movements – a kind of Corsican Mafia?'

'You could say that. Corsica is their *patrie*. Of course, they idolize Napoleon.'

Ladislav indulged me with a Czech shrug, arms outstretched, palms upward.

'In communist times, we often talked of the Seven Miracles of Czechoslovakia. The ending was:

There is nothing to be had

But you can get anything.

In spite of that, everybody steals,

And yet nothing is missing.'

THE LECTURE

The Portuguese deserve their place in the world because they never give up. I was a school director in Lisbon and we were putting a lecture on all about the Rhineland, and Herr Weltzenschmühler, our German teacher, had all his coloured slides ready.

I wasn't satisfied with the atmosphere in the lecture room, so I rang up the German Embassy and asked them to help. The voice on the phone was thoughtful, calm and to the point.

'Local colour, you want?'

'Yes. And I'd like to make it a sort of German room for the evening, if you know what I mean.'

'How many people will attend the lecture?'

'About a hundred.'

'Would you have half an hour to spare at three this afternoon, sir?

'Of course.'

'Our cultural attaché or his assistant will call on you at three, if he may.'

'That will be fine. Thank you very much.'

'*Bitte schön. Aufwiederhören.*'

You can't beat Germans for efficiency.

At a quarter to three the secretary put her head round the door.

'Mr Pereira da Silva for his appointment?'

'Send him in.'

He was middle-aged, with a black moustache. We shook hands and I steered him to a seat.

'*Sprechen Sie Deutsch?*' I asked.

His eyes widened, so I continued in Portuguese.

'Do you speak any German?'

'No, only Portuguese. Please excuse me.'

'That's all right, my German is almost as bad as my Portuguese. Did the man I spoke to on the phone explain what I wanted?'

'Oh yes, he more or less gave me your requirements. We thought it better if I came along and saw where you are going to have it.'

'Quite,' I said. I showed him the lecture room.

'It will be in here,' I told him.

'Very nice place,' he said.

We went back into my office and had a cigarette.

'Local colour,' I said. 'That is what I am after.'

'Very important,' he replied.

'As soon as they come into the room, I want them to feel that they are in the Rhineland.'

'Where?'

'The Rhineland. It's not just about Germany, you know. It's about the Rhineland in particular.'

'I see.' He took a piece of paper out of his inside jacket pocket and wrote on it.

'I think about a dozen posters would help to start off with.'

'Posters?' The idea was obviously new to him.

'What kind of posters?'

'Big ones. Coloured ones. Posters showing the boats, the hills, the Lorelei, the wine cellars, the vineyards. Get a bit of *Rheinisch* air in the place.' He was scribbling fast.

'What was that Lor . . .?'

'Lorelei. You know the place where she lured them all to a watery grave.'

He looked a little despairing. His moustache drooped.

'Can't you get one of the Lorelei?' I asked.

'I'll try,' he said.

'And maps. Do you have those?'

'Yes,' he said. 'I've got some maps.'

'You'll bring them?'

'If you like,' he said.

'Of course, we have to remember that the Rhine is not only German. It flows through Switzerland and the Netherlands, too. You wouldn't have any Swiss dolls? Or miniature Dutch windmills?'

'No,' he replied. 'We don't stock those.'

'Couldn't you manage a genuine Rüdesheim wine cask? The lecturer could put his notes on it.'

'We can try to make you one.'

He began to sketch a barrel on his paper. Rather well, I thought. I smiled and shook my head.

'We ought to bring Düsseldorf into this,' I continued. 'Have you anything of the Königsallee or Schloss Benrath?'

'Not this year,' he said.

'Couldn't you send along a couple of your people in leather shorts and green hats with feathers?'

He raised an eyebrow.

'What I mean is, we could have them distributing programmes or helping with the slides.'

He gave the gentlest of shrugs, rolled his eyes and said hoarsely, 'Well, I can always ask some of the boys. If you really think . . .'

I could see that he was not keen on it.

'You are right,' I said. 'It would be too Bavarian, not *Rheinisch*.'

'Too Bavarian,' he said.

'What about beer mugs?'

'Oh, I can get those,' he said, 'for the shelves.'

'Yes,' said I. 'I'll take the books down. A dozen of those grey ones with the coat of arms stamped on in blue and with brass lids on.'

He wrote all this down. I thought he was breathing hard.

'I'll see what I can do,' he said.

I was running short of ideas.

'I'll have Weltzenschmühler ring you up if anything else occurs to him.' We both rose to our feet and he put away his paper.

'It was very kind of you to come over,' I said. 'I'm afraid I've given you rather a tall order.'

'Not at all,' he replied. 'Of course, I'll need a few days.'

'Naturally. Do you think you can have the stuff sent over by Thursday?'

He took a deep breath and buttoned his raincoat.

'I'll try,' he said.

I went out with him to the door and on my way in again the secretary indicated a well-dressed blond gentleman sitting in the anteroom. I went over to him. He jumped smartly to his feet, smiled and shook hands.

'Schmidt,' he said, clicking his heels. 'Cultural Attaché from the German Embassy.'

'So glad you could come,' I said. 'Please take a seat while I have a word with my secretary.' He took my leather armchair and put a roll of coloured posters on my desk.

'Who was Pereira da Silva?' I asked the secretary.

'The carpenter you rang last week. You asked him to come round and take measurements for a cupboard in your office.'

'Why didn't you tell me?' I said.

'I thought you knew,' she said.

FUJITSU IN SPAIN

The well-known Japanese company Fujitsu opened a factory in Spain. The workforce was 100-strong, equally divided between Japanese and Spaniards. Besides the operatives, there were half a dozen managers of each nationality. For the first few months relations were good, then they started to deteriorate. After one year, one of the senior Spanish managers contacted me to announce that the labour force – Spaniards working side by side with Japanese – had developed a dislike for each other. As they had equal technical skills, he concluded that their mutual semi-hostility was cultural in origin. He invited me to go to Spain to look at the situation.

When I had been there for two days, I drew up a questionnaire which asked the two sides what problems they had – or thought they had – with the other. The questions touched on such matters as punctuality, courtesy, body language, diligence, leadership and so on. Typical questions were:

What do you think about the Japanese/Spanish conversation style?

What irritates you the most about the Japanese/Spaniards?

The results were surprising, enlightening, often amusing. Some comments were:

- The Spaniards are very unpunctual. They come late to work.
- The Japanese come to work hours before we do, and then they spend half the day sleeping.
- The Spaniards seem to talk all the time – but in fact they say nothing.
- The Japanese say nothing.
- The Spanish are noisy. The noise disconcerts us.
- The Japanese are silent all day. The silence is unnerving.
- The Spanish managers give orders very brusquely in a loud voice. They are not polite.
- The Japanese managers give no clear instructions. They just hint at things.
- The Spanish say they will do certain things, then they don't do them.
- The Japanese don't tell us about things, but they do them.
- The Spaniards usually begin the day making jokes and wisecracks. We don't understand them.
- The Japanese start the day by singing the company song. It was interesting for us at first but after a month it drives us crazy.
- The Spanish discuss personal matters in the office during working hours.
- The Japanese play golf in the office at lunchtime.
- The Spaniards keep touching and hugging us. Sometimes they even slap us on the back!
- The Japanese stand nearly 2 metres from us during a conversation. When we approach them in a friendly manner, they shrink away or retreat.
- You can't trust the Japanese. They won't look at you in the eye and look at their feet when talking.

- The Spaniards stare at us intensely when addressing us. You'd say they are looking into our soul.

The questionnaire had about 60 questions, and the answers revealed striking differences in how each side judged the other's behaviour. When I had digested all the comments, I arranged a two-hour session with each group of workers, explaining the behaviour of both nationalities. I also had a meeting with the managers. Practically all the problems arose from cross-cultural misunderstandings. For example, on the complaint about eye contact, I explained the following:

To the Spaniards:

'When the Japanese drop their eyes during conversation, this is a sign of humility. They are "giving you the floor", so to speak. Looking into your eyes would mean they are challenging your argument or rationale.'

When the Spaniards heard this, they showed some remorse: 'Oh, we see – humility – OK that's all right then, we misjudged them.'

To the Japanese:

'When the Spaniards seem to stare at you in an intense manner, they are in fact showing sincerity. Avoiding eye contact in Spain signifies unreliability.'

When the Japanese heard this, they were immediately contrite: 'Oh, we see – sincerity – that's quite all right then; they are not being rude at all.'

I gave an explanation of all the cultural behavioural divergences in a similar manner. Both groups showed creditable understanding and the managers told me that relations improved significantly over the following weeks.

Of course, the morning after my explanatory sessions, the

Spaniards walked around the factory and office muttering quietly as they looked at their feet, while the Japanese fixed their Spanish counterparts with intense stares of greeting and shouted 'Buenos días' at them.

TUNIS COCKTAIL PARTY

The autumn is a good time for sailing in the Mediterranean. At the end of August all the French and Italian yachts go home so that the children can go back to school. This *grande rentrée* effectively creates space in the summer-crowded marinas for those boats owned by northerners such as Scandinavians and British. In 2001 we planned an interesting itinerary for the *Ténarèze*, starting from Palermo, going west to San Vito Lo Capo, then turning south to call at Pantelleria, Lampedusa and Tunis. The route back would be Tunis–Cagliari (Sardinia)– Minorca–Majorca–Gibraltar–Algarve to our home in Vilamoura.

On board there were my wife and myself and four friends: John Antas and Ulla Saxén from Finland, and Peter Sykes (an Australian film director) and his wife Felicity from Kenya. The skipper, Ross Sneddon, was from New Zealand. It was a lively ship's company and we enjoyed the wonderful beach at San Vito, the volcanic scenery of Pantelleria and the cameo charm and African atmosphere of Lampedusa, Italy's southernmost territory. From Lampedusa the Tunisian coast was only a day's sail and we made land in Monastir, a picturesque port 130 kilometres south of Tunis. From there we made one or two inland day trips to El Jem and Kairouan, marvelling at the former's magnificent amphitheatre, arguably the best-preserved Greek monument of antiquity. After that we made our way slowly up the eastern Tunisian coast, calling at Hammamet and Sousse and eventually finding a berth in the Sidi Daoud marina, only 15 kilometres from the capital city of Tunis. There we idled a couple of days, visiting the splendid ruins of Carthage and enjoying the pleasant autumnal sunshine.

We had an interesting prospect ahead for our visit to Tunis itself. John Antas, a past president of the Lions Club in Finland, habitually contacted Lions organizations as we sailed around the world and paid the customary visits which normally included exchange of flags and brochures and, more often than not, lunch or dinner. We had previously had warm receptions in Lions Clubs in Palermo, Bari, Athens, Cape Town, Wellington, New Zealand, and Cabo Verde (where all the Lions were women!). John had never tried this stunt in an Arab country, and we looked forward to this event with no little curiosity. However, the Lions magic formula worked. John telephoned the secretary of the Tunis Lions Club and was given a warm and enthusiastic (telephonic) reception. Mr Hadidi wanted to know the number of our party along with their respective nationalities. When he heard that the visitors would be Finnish, British, Australian, Kenyan and American (my wife), his enthusiasm knew no bounds. A cocktail party would be arranged at 6pm two days later at the exclusive Tunis Tennis Club where distinguished Tunisian Lions members would receive us. The following day Hadidi visited our yacht in the marina. He was a handsome man in his mid-forties, extremely sociable and spoke good English. He spent a relaxing half hour on board, chatting with us over gin and tonics..

The next evening, we hired a chauffeur-driven seven-seater car to take us to the capital and arrived at the Tennis Club (located in an upmarket suburb) with Nordic punctuality. Hadidi had told us they had never had a Finnish Lions visitor and he was looking forward to adding the blue-and-white flag to his collection – a red-carpet reception was guaranteed. And so it turned out to be. Waiting for us in line were the Mayor of Tunis, the President of the Lions Club, the President of the Tennis Club, the Governor of the Maghreb, an important journalist for the leading Tunis newspaper, and a bright-looking younger man who interpreted between English, French and Arabic (but not Finnish).

We were greeted warmly by all these dignitaries, asked what we wanted to drink and served delightful little canapés. Remembering Hadidi's choice, we all opted for gin and tonic, as indeed did all the Tunisians except the journalist and the Maghreb gentleman, who chose soft drinks. The conversation was lively – sailing, tennis, Tunisian tourist attractions, their visits to Paris and London. Peter Sykes, in answer to questions, gave them a modest description of the wonders of Australia. The Tunisians wanted to know all about mysterious Finland, especially life in Lapland. Reindeer were compared with camels, and the Tunisian gentlemen displayed not only charming sophistication and hospitality, but also a keen sense of humour.

Things were really humming when one of the club's employees turned up the sound on the television set a few metres from the bar. The programme was, of course, in the Arabic language. As none of us understood Arabic, we glanced only idly at the screen, still conversing eagerly with our hosts. Suddenly, Peter, who was facing the TV, stiffened. John, too, twitched visibly, spilling some of his drink (most unusual for a Finn). All the Tunisians had stopped talking as the Arab commentator began to scream. We all turned our heads to find the cause, in time to see a huge jetliner crash into a tall building that bore a definite resemblance to the World Trade Center in New York City. It was September 11.

Each member of our group was searching his or her mind to think of something to say. Mesmerized by the screen, we watched dumbly as the second airliner crept into the picture from the left and traversed to crash into the second tower. All activities in the club came to a standstill; there was an eerie silence. Then words came tumbling out.

The Mayor of Tunis, as the senior person in the gathering, took the responsibility of addressing us first. He spoke well-articulated, cultivated English:

'I can assure you all that Tunisia has had nothing to do with this.'

We readily concurred (it was the obvious thing to say). The other Tunisians looked genuinely shocked apart from the Maghrebian who remained silent and the journalist who was already thinking how he would write up the event. Each man consoled the foreign guest with whom he felt most solidarity – the Lions' President put his arm round John's shoulder; the Tennis Club President commiserated with Peter and me, as he knew we were tennis players; the young interpreter, who was married to a French woman, mingled sadly with the girls. Everyone except the journalist, who looked like he wanted to be off to the office, condemned the attackers. Hadidi, obviously greatly embarrassed by the situation, blurted out a series of meaningless remarks, going from person to person, even asking John if he would like another drink.

John and Ulla lived up to the Finnish reputation for reticence, joined by my wife, who, as the only American present, considered it best to keep her mouth shut. Felicity, social creature as she was, bravely maintained the semblance of a friendly conversation with our hosts – silence would have been too hard to bear. Peter, thinking through the event and its likely repercussions, exchanged meaningful looks with me.

The Mayor, assuming correctly that our prolonged presence would lead to growing tension, delicately suggested we should all have another drink and then go on to our subsequent appointments. We were happy to be off. The journalist showed increasing signs of ambivalence vis-à-vis the attack. We suspected he derived some satisfaction from it. The interpreter was the hardest hit, the most sympathetic and anxious to be off to his wife. The senior officials were impeccably correct and saw us to our car with genuine best wishes for the continuation of our voyage. Our driver was tight-lipped as we returned to the boat. Our mobile phones rang constantly during the trip. Our son, Italian friends, and various Finns and Australians rang us to find out where we were. When we told them Tunisia, they all advised us to get the hell out.

Back on board, we discovered that Ross had heard nothing about the attack. He was shocked.

'Perhaps it's better if we leave tomorrow morning early,' I ventured.

'We can't,' replied Ross, 'I've just sent the mainsail to the sailmaker's for repair.'

'When do we get it back?'

'In three days. The 14th.'

We digested this information. The Tunisian employees in the marina, as well as spectators who frequently came along the quay to admire the Tenareze, our Finnish Swan yacht, were all behaving normally, even showing friendliness. But, as they say, three days is a long time in politics.

'The American revenge will be devastating,' I offered. Peter, world-wise, concurred completely. In the back of our minds was the notion of what might happen if Bush retaliated by bombing Mecca. Unlikely, but not unthinkable. We looked at our masthead guest flags and after dark, lowered the American and Australian ones. The uncontroversial Finnish flag we left up.

In a way, we sweated it out for three days, paying several visits to the sailmakers to see if the job was being done. We need not have feared: his politics were what they were, but he made money out of fixing sails. We departed late morning on the 14th under Finnish colours, in golden sunshine and setting course for Cagliari, Sardinia. The Finnish and Tunisian Lions Clubs still maintain friendly relations but have not exchanged visits since that memorable day. We left with a favourable impression of Tunisian culture, hospitality and adaptability.

7

INDONESIAN IN FINLAND

Mattila's company sent him out to Indonesia, where for three years he enjoyed continuous sunshine, exotic food and the company of black-haired, dark-eyed women. Blond Finnish men in their late twenties tend to fall for this type of beauty, and Mattila was no exception. Six months before leaving Indonesia, he married Mona, a charming, lively young schoolteacher of 25. They went to Penang for their honeymoon, staying in the famous Rasa Sayang Hotel. It was the first time Mona had been outside Indonesia.

Returning to Finland, Mattila was posted to Kauhava, a small town in the western part of the country. Kauhava is clean and well laid out and enjoys fresh air and good snow in winter, but it is not one of Finland's most exciting towns. Mona did not play tennis or ski – in fact, she had never seen snow. The local theatre company played in Finnish. She could watch some English-language films on TV, but in general her avenues for entertainment were severely limited. On top of that, Mattila knew hardly anybody in Kauhava. Finns in a new location tend to make friends slowly and somewhat cautiously.

In spite of their taciturn exteriors, however, most Finns have hearts of gold, though it may take strangers months, or even years, to discover this. The good citizens of Kauhava perceived the predicament in which Mattila, and more especially Mona, found themselves. One of Mattila's neighbours took the bull by the horns, and actually knocked on Mattila's door and introduced himself. He told Mattila that a ring of neighbours – about a dozen of them – had discussed the matter and had resolved to hold a welcome party for the young couple. They fixed a date – the following Wednesday evening at 6pm. Mattila gratefully accepted the offer. Mona was agog with excitement.

The following Wednesday Mona put on her dancing shoes and her party dress – an explosion of colour amid the drab grey of Kauhava's dwellings – and, arm in arm with her husband, tripped gaily up to the house chosen for the party. A nice little sign 'WELCOME TO KAUHAVA' had been rigged up at the front door. Mona took a picture of it.

Inside the house the partygoers had formed a disciplined symmetry. The owner of the house took Mona and Mattila round, introducing each couple. The men shook hands rather stiffly, Mona thought, bowing slightly as they proffered their names: Lehtonen, Lahtinen, Virtanen, Kunnas . . . some clicked their heels. The wives also extended their hands, smiling more openly than the men, some getting closer as if they were going to kiss Mona, though no one did.

Introductions completed, the host assigned comfortable seats to those who did not wish to stand. Most of the men drank gin and tonics standing. Ladies sat with white wines or rum-colas. Mona drank beer. Small, delicious canapés were served; everybody settled down in groups of three or four, conversing in low tones. Occasional bursts of laughter punctuated the exchanges. Most of the ladies had their turn with Mona, asking how she liked Kauhava and Finland, commenting on her colourful attire. The men sneaked interested glances at her from a distance, but became shier when nearer. Time passed, drinks were freshened, everyone scrutinized a couple of Thai prints on one of the walls. Mona noticed that several of the men were capable of maintaining 10 minutes' silence or even half an hour. The women were more talkative, in brief bursts. Monologues were obviously taboo.

After a couple of hours, during which a considerable amount of alcohol was consumed by the men, who showed some signs of controlled inebriation, Mona sidled up to Mattila and whispered in his ear:

'When is the party going to begin?'

The remark took Mattila completely by surprise. Drawing Mona slightly to one side, he whispered fiercely, 'It's nearly finished.'

'But nobody has announced anything and what about the entertainment? It's so quiet.'

'Shh . . . they're all enjoying themselves.'

Not long after, the first couples left, politely taking leave of Mona with firm handshakes. 'Come round and see us. You can have a sauna.'

Mona suppressed a shudder and smiled at each couple:

'Thank you, it was a lovely party.'

'Don't worry, there will be plenty more.'

8

NEXT, PLEASE!

The fashion firm Next™ sold their clothes in 39 foreign locations and asked me for cultural advice on several occasions. I visited their headquarters in Leicester and had discussions with their design and sales department. At HQ they had a central showroom as big as a medium-sized dance hall. Twice a year – in spring and in autumn – they would line the walls of the room with all their new fashions displayed on coat hangers. You could peruse shirts, dresses, trousers, skirts, pullovers, blouses – the entire production since the last show six months earlier. To this exhibition they would invite 39 buyers from the countries where they had shops.

Starting at bottom right, one of the top saleswomen would conduct an *anti-clockwise* tour of the items of clothing, pointing out novelties and other interesting features and answering any questions posed to her. The tour of the room took about 40 minutes. I thought it was a very practical way of exhibiting their new models: they dealt with all 39 of their foreign colleagues in one go, any queries could be dealt with there and then. The foreign buyers seemed very pleased with the system, following the saleswomanl round, a happy, eager, homogeneous bunch.

Next had warned me that there was an anomaly on such occasions. One of the foreign buyers started the tour bottom left and went round *clockwise*, alone. Naturally, she did not benefit from the guidance and explanations of the models given by the rather sophisticated saleswoman. In the first few years, people from Next had tried to persuade the lone buyer (it was sometimes a man and sometimes a woman) to join the group: it would be more edifying, not to mention sociable, they said, and just think of all the little bits of information you are missing.

'No, thank you. I am perfectly able to make my own mind up, thank you.'

And so it went every year. Thirty-eight buyers and the saleswoman always met and crossed with the lone buyer at the halfway point, smiles or nods were exchanged, and everyone finished at the same time.

And who was the maverick? The Finn, of course. This did not surprise me, but Next was interested to know the roots of this behaviour. I told them that Finns, more than any other Europeans, have a strong streak of independence. Furthermore, they do not like being hovered over. In Helsinki, customers are not followed around by sales assistants in shops. If they were, they would tell the followers to go away. Finns find persuasive shop assistants in Paris or Milan extremely irritating. They are capable of being rude to them. Never try to persuade a Finn to do or buy anything. Arm-twisting is taboo in Finland.

One of the Next managers laughed, understanding well what I meant. Her eyes twinkled and she leaned over to give me another piece of news.

'Mr Lewis, last autumn, we had a new development.'

'You did?'

'A second person joined the clockwise tour. Now there are two of them.'

I thought for a moment and returned: 'And I can tell you the nationality of the second person.'

'You can?'

'Estonian.'

'Absolutely correct, but how did you know?'

'Estonians have the same independent streak as the Finns. And they would take pleasure in showing they could be equally awkward. Like the Finns, they speak an Asiatic language. Their thought grooves are similar. They were showing Finno-Ugrian solidarity.'

'Well, well.'

'I bet they are two of your best customers.'

'They are indeed!'

'Then you have nothing to worry about.'

THE MISSING SHOES

A few years ago, I was working and living in Tokyo and was honoured by a visit from Helge, a Swedish friend of mine, who was representing the Axel Johnson concern. He brought with him a Swedish engineer, Lennart, to help him with the Japanese assignment.

On their first evening in Tokyo, I took Helge and Lennart to a well-known Japanese restaurant (the Furusato) which featured a two-hour programme of folkloric singing and dancing. Customers sat, of course, on tatami floors and shoes had to be left in the entrance hall. People living in Japan are used to this system, and Helge had been to Tokyo before; Lennart, however, was on his first visit and was reluctant to take his shoes off. What if someone took them? It never happens in Japan, I assured him. But he had long, narrow Swedish feet and would not be able to find any suitable replacements in Tokyo if his own shoes vanished. I had never heard of any foreigner having his shoes stolen from the entrance hall of the Japanese-style restaurant, I insisted, particularly not from a high-class establishment like the Furusato. Helge added weight to my argument, and finally Lennart, not without misgiving, took off his Swedish shoes and attended the show in his stockinged feet.

The singing and dancing were most entertaining, the food was excellent. At 10pm we paid the bill and went to the entrance hall. Lennart's shoes were missing. Not mine, not Helge's, not anybody else's, just Lennart's. He made a stink. Waiters, waitresses, doormen, the restaurant manager, were rushing everywhere. They showed Lennart the 40 remaining pairs of shoes, twice or three times. None were his. The manager was particularly upset, almost as much as Lennart. He had a fistful of yen for Lennart and offered to finance any pair of shoes in Tokyo. This had never happened in his 25 years of management of the Furusato. He bowed till his back ached.

Lennart took a taxi back to the Okura Hotel wearing a pair of Furusato slippers and spent the next two days trying to find a pair of shoes that would fit him. He was a size 12 and had to do his shopping wearing slippers. He missed several business appointments and in the end had his wife send his best pair from Sweden by SAS. The whole thing was a disaster.

Twenty years later, Helge was dying in Stockholm and I went to visit him. He was reasonably comfortable, and I had a wonderful dinner in his home with him, his wife and daughter. We reminisced about old times.

Late in the evening, Helge leaned forward over his coffee and addressed me with a glint in his eye.

'Do you remember the night in Tokyo when Lennart had his shoes stolen?'

'I most certainly do. I'll never forget it.'

'Do you remember how he had to go all over Tokyo in slippers?'

'I do.'

Helge smiled devilishly and said to me:

'I took those shoes. I slipped out to go to the toilet and hid them under a bush in the front garden.'

'You did?'

'Yes, and the next morning I went back and got them. I kept them for 10 years and then sent them to Lennart as a present for his 50th birthday.'

Helge was a great, intensely humorous Swede, though I doubt the poor manager of the Furusato would ever agree with me.

10

GUESTS OF THE STATE

Twenty-first-century Spain still provides cross-cultural delights for Northern Europeans and Americans. It was also true of Franco's Spain of 1949, though one had to tread carefully.

In that year, as I was studying Spanish with Professor Geoffrey Stagg, the eminent Cervantes scholar at Nottingham University, I decided to make my debut visit to Spain and asked Arthur, my school and university friend, to come with me. He was a bit hesitant at first, as he spoke no Spanish and was only 5 foot 4, but he was a great footballer and 5 foot 4 was reasonably tall in Andalusia, so when I had taught him some basic phrases – 'thank you', 'good-bye' and 'my friend will pay' – he agreed to come. We had a great six weeks travelling around, acquainting ourselves with bullfights, tapas, *tintos*, olives, churros, pelota, flamenco, chorizo, *tortilla de patata*, museums and art galleries. Arthur dazzled young Spaniards footballing on the beach. Filling in Franco's *tripticos* – residence forms to be filled in in triplicate every night was – less exciting.

Our last day in Spain was supposed to be Friday, when we took the train from Barcelona to the French frontier. We were slightly weary of cross-cultural encounters of the Franco kind, but on balance we thought Spain and the Spaniards were great.

On the Friday morning we bought train tickets to Cerbère, the first French town over the border as one travels north. We were due in Cerbère at 9pm and decided to have dinner there. Lunch we took in the dining car, making the most of our last Spanish meal by using up our remaining pesetas. We ate *jamón de York* for starters, moving on to a fine leg of lamb (*cordero asado*), goat's cheese from Navarra and *crema catalana* as dessert. When we had paid the bill, we went through all our pockets, seeking any surviving pesetas, which we piled up on the table for Arthur to count. Arthur has this thing about never changing money twice. He calculates in advance what he needs, changes that amount, then metes it out to the last centavo. He seldom runs short, but he hates to be left over with any. He once had 10 cents left in Swiss money as his train was about to leave Switzerland, and he bought a pair of shoelaces in the kiosk on the platform.

On this occasion he decided we had enough for another dessert (we loved *crema catalana*), coffees and two or three cognacs each to pass away the time as the train crawled towards the frontier. We seemed to halt longer in each station as the afternoon wore on, and as falling dusk accompanied our last budgeted drink, we began to realize that dinner might be late that night. In the event, we arrived at Portbou, the Spanish border town, at 10pm and the frontier with France had closed for the night. We were told that a train would go through the tunnel the next day, Saturday, at noon.

Our problem was that we had no Spanish money left. We had pounds, but the law at the time forbade us to change any, except in the bank, which would be closed the next morning. Portbou banks barely make it on weekdays. Spanish restaurateurs and hotelkeepers were not allowed to receive foreign currency, and, even if they had done, we would have had problems with the currency declaration. On entering Spain, you filled in a form declaring the amount you had in pounds and francs. That amount you had to take out again, minus whatever a bank receipt showed you had changed officially. It all sounds trivial today, when you can change money freely even on the black market. It was quite a different matter in Spain in 1949, when they checked every document three times and where any petty discrepancy was swooped on by officials desperate to relieve the boredom of their unproductive occupation.

Arthur had got us down to two pesetas, and I daresay I was a little cool with him as hunger returned. We went into the Café Central to make our plans.

'What shall we do?' I asked Arthur.

We were drinking coffee so we were already in the red. Arthur stared at reflected lights in the glass-topped table while he considered the alternatives. He had that calm, contemplative look on his face, which he wore when he was picking football teams.

'Let's change a pound – enough for dinner, hotel room, and breakfast and souvenirs tomorrow morning.'

'What about the Customs? No banks, no receipts. No receipts, no leave Spain. You know how it is, Arthur.'

'Leave the Customs to me,' he said.

Arthur, now in charge, beckoned to the café bootblack, an old wrinkled fellow with a conspiratorial air, to come over and shine my shoes. Catching on quickly, I sneaked a pound note out of my back pocket and slipped it to the bootblack muttering the useful word *cambio*. He took the money without taking his eyes off my shoes, and I stared at the crowd like the great bullfighter Manolete on a lucky day. Arthur thought we both did it rather well. The old man went off on his errand and returned 10 minutes later to clean Arthur's shoes. Once he had the pesetas Arthur paid him off and ordered supper for two. It was 11pm.

I was still worried about receipts, but when two pork chops were put in front of me, I decided to give them the concentration they deserved. When I had eaten one, an unshaven character came in from the street and tried to sell us half a dozen Parker 51s for the price of a good meal. I sent him off. Halfway through the second chop another stubbly chin came to the table and offered to guide us over the hill to France for 100 pesetas apiece. No Customs up there, he explained.

We were in the middle of our dessert when the police came in and arrested us. There were three of them with guns. One would have been enough. We went quietly. They did not give us time to pay the bill. I thought they would march us up to the police station, but we all did it at a stroll. Once inside, we were relieved of our rucksacks and told to present our passports to the sergeant. He was a mean-looking, bull-necked Galician with the crisp singsong accent of that province. Without opening the passports, he put them on his desk and charged us with suspected smuggling of Parker pens and trying to make an illegal exit from Spain after the closure of the frontier.

I broke the news to Arthur, who did not take it well at all. If he had not been well fed, I think he would have come out with something which would have got us in even more trouble with the sergeant. As it was, I made no impression on him with Stagg's Spanish, and soon he was ordering his subordinates to lock up our rucksacks in cupboards and making us sign slips of paper left and right. When he eventually deigned to look inside our passports, he said they were out of order. Tomorrow we would be sent back to Madrid. Nobody mentioned changing pound notes.

They took us across the road to a white building with thick walls and no windows. We were allocated separate rooms, about 3 metres by 2. My room had nothing in it but a bed, a bible and a cockroach. At least there were no bars. The room had an ordinary wooden door which our guard closed but left unlocked. We would be questioned further at 8.30, he said.

After lying on my cot for a while wondering who had turned us in, I slept fitfully for a couple of hours and awoke to some sound in the corridor. I decided I would go and confer with Arthur regarding the morrow. The door creaked slightly as I tiptoed into the corridor. Facing me was the dim shape of a guardia in his melancholy three-cornered hat, a carbine across his knees. He looked at me questioningly. I asked him where the conveniences were. He escorted me there, stood with me, then accompanied me back to my quarters. The next morning, Arthur told me he had gone through the same ceremony. The guard could not have had a very good night, either. Arthur had offered him a cigarette, but he had just shaken his head and tapped his gun significantly with two fingers. Arthur supposed he meant he could not smoke while on duty.

Under the circumstances, we rose early, and our guard took us into a nearby private house where a wizened old woman gave us coffee and rolls for five pesetas. Arthur offered the guard another cigarette after breakfast. This time he accepted it and stowed it carefully in the top pocket of his tunic. He escorted us to the police station at 8.30 for our questioning, but the sergeant was in bed and was not to be disturbed. The young corporal on duty motioned us to sit down and we waited around an hour and a half, during which time the corporal tried four of Arthur's 'Sweet Virginias'. '*Muy rubio,*' he kept saying – very blond tobacco. At ten o' clock he unlocked the cupboard where our rucksacks were and restituted our property against the usual slips of paper. He then found our passports and, after a brief scrutiny, passed them across the counter. We could go, he said, but there would be problems with the Customs.

Arthur left him the rest of his fags, and the corporal saluted us as we made our exit. We walked down the street to the harbour and looked at the clear water sparkling in the morning sunlight. The sun was warm on our backs and Arthur suggested I had a swim. He never swims before noon, so I took him at his word and went in without him. As I swam up and down, I could see Arthur sitting there thinking. I remembered his offer to deal with the Customs. At half past eleven, Arthur bought three bananas, eating one himself and giving me another. Then he sent an urchin down to the station to see what time the train to France would leave. The boy returned and informed that it would depart half an hour late, at half past twelve. Arthur gave him one peseta and the remaining banana.

I was getting anxious to go to the station, but Arthur pulled me the other way up the main street. We went into the bar where we had eaten the previous evening, and Arthur paid the bill. The proprietor was so glad to see us that he set out two cognacs on the house. We drank these, and Arthur ordered two more and one for the proprietor.

After that some of the customers joined in and our pesetas dwindled rapidly. At 12.25, we heard the engine whistle go and the first laboured puffs of the locomotive. Arthur gulped down his brandy, grabbed me by the sleeve and we ran pell-mell down the street to the station 50 metres away. When we arrived on the platform the engine had just put its head into the black mouth of the tunnel and 10 wooden carriages were heading slowly after it. There was no time for passports or currency receipts or dignified embarkations. Customs officials and rail-waymen shouted and waved their arms wildly, as they ran along the platform with us. One got a door open, a second pushed us in and a third threw in our rucksacks after us.

'*Gracias*,' shouted Arthur as we waved goodbye. I looked at him. As they sometimes say, a little language goes a long way.

11

DANISH IS GOOD FOR YOU

The cultural gap between English people and Danes is a rather narrow one. The two peoples get on well together, and misunderstandings are few. It also seems that the Danish sense of humour is closer to the English than anyone else's. The only problem English people have with Danes is when they have a cross-cultural encounter with the Danish language.

Let me explain. At university, I was studying Spanish and French, but, on account of my good relations with Professor Stagg, who taught both Spanish and Italian, I was able to take Italian as an extra subject.

Beegan, one of my friends from the poker crowd, was doing a degree in German and had found that Danish as an extra language in the linguistics stream obviated the need for studying many thick tomes of German literature, which meant more time for poker. Danish was a bit of a lark, so he asked me to join him for company.

My experience in the Danish lectures served to illustrate my belief that, while learning a language can be an easy and painless task, in certain circumstances things can go awfully wrong, even with good linguists. Professor Clark was Professor of German, but he was proud of his Danish, too. His enthusiasm infected us, and we made good progress in the first term, attending lessons three times a week. Soon we were gambolling through Hans Christian Andersen's fairy tales in the original, and by Christmas we were telling each other jokes in Danish. Beegan was using it for poker. Clark was delighted.

For the Christmas term Professor Clark was due to lecture at the University of Copenhagen, and the Danes were sending us a Danish professor in exchange. This seemed a good idea to everybody at the time. The Danish professor was in his late thirties, wore a white shirt and bowtie, and exuded Viking energy. He seemed glad to have got out of Denmark. The first day that he took us he introduced himself as Professor Hansen and said that his colleague Clark had told him he could conduct the course entirely in Danish since we had already been chatting away in it for three months. We all concurred, and Professor Hansen continued the lecture in Danish. After 20 minutes Beegan stopped him.

'*Hvad er det for noget?*' asked the professor.

'Please, sir, nobody understands a single word.'

You had to hand it to Beegan – he wasn't one to beat about the bush. Professor Hansen looked a little upset, but he took it well in the end.

'Not a single word?'

'Not a single one.'

'But Professor Clark said you speak Danish.'

'We do, sir. But we can't understand it.'

'But didn't you understand Professor Clark?'

'Yes, sir. But it isn't the same.'

'What isn't the same?'

'It isn't the same Danish, sir.'

'Not the same Danish?'

'No, sir.'

'But surely . . . there is only one Danish. I mean, after all . . . Danish is Danish!'

'Professor Clark has his own, sir.'

'But what is this Danish like?'

'Do you wish me to read some, sir?'

'Yes, please do.'

Beegan began to read from his Danish book, and we all began to understand again. But the professor stopped him after five lines. He looked sorry for Beegan and asked somebody else to read and then a third . . . After that he couldn't take any more. He suggested coffee for everybody in the refectory, and we broke up for the morning.

For the rest of the term he gave us pronunciation drill. It is only the pronunciation that makes Danish difficult. Andersen's fairy tales were familiar to us and we could read them in Danish at will, only rarely having to consult the dictionary for the odd word. But it was all in the mind. It was a phonetic dream. Professor Hansen's Danish from Copenhagen was a new, alien and at times almost terrifying phenomenon. It could have been Martian. What was worse, it was practically inimitable. Some of us were not too bad as linguists go, and we were well aware of the value of slavish imitation of a native speaker. I daresay most of us would have made a fairly respectable attempt at *un bon vin blanc*. But Hansen said things like *rød grød med flød* (red porridge with cream), and we could not say it like he did for all the bacon in Denmark.

After a while he abandoned the idea of our being able to pronounce whole sentences correctly and started concentrating on short phrases. These, too, proved to be beyond our reach and he soon relegated us to single words and subsequently to separate syllables. The final ignominy came when we were struggling with our vocal mechanism to produce a simple Danish sound like ø for instance.

There was not, Hansen told us, just one ø sound in Danish. There were three. There was ø and there was ø and there was ø.

The Swedes tell you the same thing, except that they say there is ö and ö and ö. All you have to do is distinguish between them. Professor Hansen could do it. He used to say them slowly for us, one after the other. To make it easier for us, he numbered the three different sounds. This simple table helped us a lot:

1	2	3
ø	ø	ø

If he had not numbered them, there would have been the danger of our not knowing which was which.

If you don't know what ø sounds like, Beegan used to say that it was more or less the sound a burly Scot emits when he tosses the caber. Especially ø number 2. No. 2 was Beegan's speciality. He could always say no. 2. I used to be pretty good at no. 1 myself, and O'Flaherty never failed on no. 3. This was the sort of conversation which took place during the pronunciation drill:

Hansen: Beegan, give us the second ø, will you please?

Beegan: Ø.

Hansen: Excellent! Now give us no. 3.

Beegan: Ø.

Hansen: Tsk, tsk, Beegan, that was no. 2 again. O'Flaherty, you give us no. 3.

O'Flaherty: Ø.

Hansen: Well done, my boy. Beegan, try again on no. 3.

Beegan: Ø.

Hansen: No, no, you're back on no. 2 again!

Beegan: Sorry, sir.

It is hard for anyone who has never heard Danish spoken to imagine just what sounds can be produced by even an average Dane, let alone a professor. I suspect they all have cleft palates or some kind of equivalent. We couldn't hope to match them with our ordinary palates. Beegan made a fair show of counting up to six, but he found *syv* (seven) unpronounceable. Hansen had O'Flaherty a whole week trying to say *dage* (days). When O'Flaherty said 'days' in English he was nearer to the correct Danish pronunciation than he was when he was when he tried to say it in Danish, so Hansen finally let him say it in English. Beegan just refused the gate with *halvtresindstyve* (fifty). When Professor Hansen returned to Copenhagen at the end of term, he left an unfinished task behind him. He had taken great pains to make something out of us, and he had not always seen the fruits of his labour.

The departure of Professor Hansen heralded the return of Professor Clark, and the opening of the summer term brought with it a sneaking nostalgia for our old fairy tales. It was like old times when we saw his familiar figure shuffle in through the doorway and pad up to his desk, the beloved book under his arm. We skipped through the pages, expectantly.

As he opened his tattered copy, we noticed the tired lines under his eyes, and we could detect a new humility in his glance. The poor old boy had had as rough a time of it as we had. He, too, had been through the mill.

Finally, he found the right page, and he started reading the opening paragraph of the tale. He had a poker face. O'Flaherty looked at Beegan and Beegan looked at me. For some moments the guttural stream of alien syllables swirling around our ears stunned us – numbed our thought process. Then slowly it dawned on us, and, looking at our teacher with new eyes, we knew that the good old days had gone for ever.

Professor Clark had gone over to the other side.

GREENLAND – WHY IS CULTURE SO DEEPLY ROOTED?

Culture is deeply embedded. A Danish colleague of mine recently went to give a one-week intensive English language course to a group of Greenlandic fishermen. The programme was jointly sponsored by the Danish Ministry of Education and the Greenland Department of Tourism. The students, 20-strong (mixed Inuit and Danish blood) were almost beginners in English but keen.

My Danish friend was beginning to develop the feeling that she understood Greenlandic behaviour, though not of course the language. Greenlanders have enjoyed a long association with Denmark and have obviously absorbed some Danish characteristics such as a keen sense of humour, tolerance of other cultures, a healthy respect for learning and education, and a rather easy-going nature. The teacher noticed nothing different in the way they reacted to instruction from that typical of Danish students. For two days, they practised attentively.

Suddenly, on the third morning of lessons, one of them near the window sniffed, muttered five words in East Greenlandic, and the whole group rushed out of the room and disappeared for half an hour. They then returned to their seats and awaited further instruction. When my colleague asked what had caused them to depart so suddenly, they explained that the wind had changed. They all had had to move their boats.

The next day lessons were in full swing when a Greenlander stuck his head through the door and shouted five more words. The entire group rushed out again, but they did not come back this time. When the teacher, curious, eventually followed them outside to find out what was happening, she saw them all on the beach (with the rest of the village) pulling in a whale. For the next few hours the whole community was feverishly occupied in cutting up the huge animal into a large number of pieces and putting these into barrels and buckets. It was 20 degrees below zero and dark (January). They all went home to wash the blood off themselves and came back to the lesson at 10pm. Normal behaviour.

RATS IN CHONGQING

In the spring of 1985 we decided to undertake a cycle ride along the Yangtse River, from Chongqing in the west, to Shanghai at its southern estuary.

We were a party of nine: Jane and I and our three children, Caroline, Richard and David; Diane, an American college friend of Jane; Mathias Wallen and Anna Mattila from Finland; and Kimi Morizane, a 17-year-old Japanese boy, a friend of the family.

The plan was first to fly to Beijing, spend a few days there, then to fly west the length of China to Chongqing, and then cycle down the Yangtse to Shanghai on the east coast. This we achieved in due course. The following describes our first day in Chongqing before we embarked on our month-long cycle ride.

We arrived in brilliant sunshine, though it was already five in the afternoon. China International Travel Service (CITS) met us regally at the airport, and the two guides, a young man and a young woman, both speaking creditable English, helped us and our bags into a rickety green-and-white bus for the one-hour ride to the Chongqing Grand Hotel. We rattled through innumerable suburbs – rural rather than urban in nature. Pigs and chickens were everywhere, with cats and dogs in suspiciously short supply. Even the outlying districts seemed thronged with people – astonished faces peeped out at us from every alleyway, window and hole in the wall. Foreigners were a common sight in Beijing and Shanghai in 1985; they were still a rarity on the Upper and Middle Yangtse.

On coming into what appeared to be the city centre, our guides asked the bus driver to stop the vehicle. The male guide flung out his right arm over a valley-like park and indicated a palatial-looking building, 200 metres long, on the other side.

'That, ladies and gentlemen, is the Grand Hotel – your hotel for tonight,' he intoned proudly.

We were impressed. Not only did it rival the Escorial and the Mafra Palace in length, but it was of the classic architecture of Chinese antiquity. In fact, as I realized later, it was a carbon copy of the Palace of Heaven in Beijing. We thanked the CITS for providing us with such sumptuous accommodation, bearing in mind our cramped quarters in Beijing. Our vision of royal apartments to wallow in luxury in was, of course, both naive and short-lived. At the check-in desk we were assigned two rooms, though one of them was, we were told, quite sizeable. Six and three was the split. What to do with five men and four women? The clerk was surprised at our lack of invention: one woman would go in with five men, naturally.

Of course, Jane joined us males – at least there were four beds – and Caroline, Diane and Anna took the other room, which already had one inhabitant – a young English university student backpacking her way through China. The two rooms were both on the front of the hotel and were at opposite ends of the 200-yard terrace with its magnificent balustrade. They were dingy in the extreme, but the huge columns of the balustrade reminded us of past imperial glory.

Chongqing is the largest city in Sichuan Province, noted for its wonderful, very spicy cuisine. After settling in, we went to a restaurant recommended by our guides and had what turned out to be the very best meal we encountered in China. It was the local speciality – a monstrous river fish cooked in a variety of spices and then coated from head to tail in chocolate! There were lots of piquant side dishes too, but that huge fish lives in my memory. Nine of us could not finish it off.

We wandered round the streets and side-alleys of Chongqing until midnight. The houses were small, often one or two storeys, the great majority were wooden or corrugated-iron lean-tos against supporting brick walls. People beckoned us to inspect the interiors. I am really not sure why. Either they wanted to shame us (for living so well, when they lived so humbly) or they were simply being friendly and had man's natural incli-nation to invite people into his home. In most cases they lived six to eight in the only room, with a few animals thrown in. They washed their babies and small children in enamel basins full of tepid brown water, usually out on the street in front of their dwelling. At 11pm nobody seemed to be in bed – children, grown-ups and animals milled around. In some houses 20 or 30 people gathered around TV sets, volume turned up to maximum.

I will not dwell further on the poverty, the inhuman over-crowding, the smells, the unbelievable absence of any pretence of hygiene. These facts are often mentioned when one describes China. Suffice it to say that it is far more demeaning than one can imagine (at least in cities like Chongqing), yet these people bore themselves with dignity, often with gentleness. In every-one's eyes – miraculously – one detected a glimmer of hope.

We all went to bed around 1am, weary from sensory overload, sensing the throbbing pulse of rural–urban China, her enormous problems, her 16-hour-day-long energy, her compulsive industriousness, her age-old wisdom and perceptiveness, her invincible durability. The hotel rooms were dark, for electricity was cut off around midnight – it saved money. We groped around for our beds and belongings, soon hit our respective pillows. After half an hour, the six of us were rudely awakened by terrified female screams and the thudding of feet. Our door, carefully fastened for security, was battered on frenziedly. Kimi, nearest to it, opened it dizzily. Caroline, Anna and Diane, silhouetted in the pale moonlight, came stumbling over the threshold.

'Rats!' they yelled.

We fumbled for our torches and finally threw some light on the events occurring in the other room. The girls had been woken up after a few minutes' sleep by rodents crawling over them. Anna thought that it was Caroline giving her a friendly paw and touched a warm rat in the dark. There were plenty of others.

Caroline, Anna and Diane made it clear they were definitely not going back, not even to collect their belongings. I am no great rat-tamer myself, but somebody had to go and check things out. I took the biggest of the torches and walked the length of the balustrade to Room 9. The door was still wide open and, as I poked my torch through the opening, the beam illuminated a dozen rodents scampering up and down on the three empty beds. On the fourth bed, snoring soundly and with not a care in the world, was the young woman from Nottingham University, one rat perched on her chest and two others strolling round her. I didn't see any point in waking her – she obviously could handle things in China. I swept my beam here and there and grabbed rucksacks and sleeping bags, which I threw out on the balcony. A dozen pairs of beady rat eyes, reflecting luminous red in my direction, watched me contemptuously. Not one animal showed any fear of me – they were dead right. Few men would have tackled a dozen of them with one torch. I was not one of them.

We were now nine in a room – that is to say, at least nine, for whether or not we were also cohabiting with rodents in Room 2 had yet to be established. Nine powerful torches swept over every nook and cranny. Nobody seemed sleepy any more. Mathias, Jane and I were the only ones who had ever seen rats before – he on the farm, Jane in the suburbs of Buenos Aires, and I running along the railway lines in Wigan station. We finally decided Room 2 was OK, though Mathias put his two apples in the pockets of his anorak, which he hung up on a hook to make sure no rodents got them. We all had an undisturbed night – nobody saw or heard a single rat or mouse. But the next morning Mathias's pockets contained only apple cores.

The next morning, I decided to test some of the Chinese qualities which the inhabitants of the Middle Kingdom said they possessed. On check-out I asked for our combined bill and, on receiving it, asserted I would only pay half. The clerk looked me in the eye uncomprehendingly.

'Why only half?' he queried.

'We were only nine. There were at least 18 of us in Rooms 2 and 9 – perhaps more.'

'Eighteen, sir?'

'Rats. They shared our rooms.'

'Rats, sir?'

I thought he was playing the hypocrite, but then he reached for his dictionary and I held my fire.

'L-A-T, sir?'

'No, R-A-T.'

'I see,' he found the word. He avoided my eye, but nodded

quietly and went off to find the manager, who soon appeared. They exchanged views quickly in voluble Sichuanese. The manager looked at me apologetically and smiled gently.

'It's all right, sir – you can pay half.'

Honest people, I thought. And in fact, we encountered no dishonesty while we were in China. I guess that's what cross-culture is all about.

BIKES IN CHINA

We bought nine bicycles for our trip, all identical. They were rather heavy, black, sit-up-and-beg style, and had only one gear, no lamps or bells, and cost about £50 each, which we thought very reasonable. The police told us that we would need number plates for each one. As they told us it would take three weeks to obtain them, we decided to leave without. China's new 'paramount leader', Deng Xiaoping, had recently instructed the population to be nice to foreigners. We felt we could take the risk. In the event, we were never stopped by the police, although a few officers glared at us from time to time.

I do not have enough space in this book to describe in detail the many adventures we encountered along our six-week ride along the Yangtse, but one incident is worth telling, as it illustrates a problem we frequently had in 'getting lost'.

One day the twisting and heavily built-up road we were riding along, departed from the river a considerable distance and we could not find it again. None of us spoke Chinese, and the large group of Chinese youngsters following us on their bikes did not understand we were lost. As we tried to make ourselves clear, an elderly gentleman also on a bike approached us and said, 'I speak a little English.'

We told him we were looking for the river. He looked at me and spoke two words:

'Follow me.'

He cycled off and we followed, accompanied by our 100-strong entourage of youngsters. After 15 minutes the elderly gentleman led us to the Yangtse, which we were glad to see again as it was our route to Shanghai.

I asked the kind old gentleman, 'How did you learn English?'

'Follow me!' he replied.

This was the name of the famous BBC series 'Teaching English by Television'.

After a fascinating though somewhat exhausting ride along the Yangtse, we decided to sell the bikes in Suzhou – only an hour's train ride from Shanghai – rather than tackle this sprawling metropolis from the saddle. The cycles were all in good condition, and we figured that, if we offered them at half the price we had paid for them, we should get ready takers. This turned out to be true, though we were not sure how we should go about the business. The CITS guide wanted nothing to do with it, as he was not sure of the legal position.

We hummed and hawed a while. Finally, I lined them all up outside a jewellery shop on one of the main streets and shouted, 'Bicycles for sale!' In the space of two minutes we were surrounded by inquisitive passers-by. Once the word had got round that we were selling bikes, people started producing money. The price of a new bicycle represents many months of salary for most Chinese, so the chance to get a near-new one at half-price meant there was no haggling. It took people about half an hour to assemble the cash, then one bike went, then a second, then a third and a fourth. I was stuffing wads of dirty banknotes into my pockets till they could hold no more – we were soon going to need a suitcase.

Just when the business was going well, the police arrived – at least one constable did. The crowds parted to leave a corridor for him. He strode quickly forward, grabbed a bike by the handlebars, wheeled it round in a circle, looked for the registration plate which wasn't there, then addressed me sharply in singsong Shanghainese. I nodded dumbly. Then he bought the bike and pedalled off on it.

There was pandemonium in the crowd over the last four bikes. The jeweller and his son dashed out of their shop, grabbed two of them, wheeled them into the shop and beckoned me inside. He took me to the till and emptied it, spreading the money over the glass-topped counter. There was not enough – the day's takings could only buy one and a half bikes. He gave me various messages in Shanghainese and sign language and his son high-tailed it out of the shop in order (as I understood) to fetch the remaining cash. Other people were now waving money at me through the glass door, which the jeweller kept firmly locked. After 10 minutes his son came back and completed the purchase.

Mathias and the boys were trying to hang on to the remaining two bikes, but in the milling throng, two men seized them and pedalled off with them. We shouted at them irately in several languages, but they disappeared in the dusk. The crowd laughed uproariously; we felt pretty sick at this point but stuffed our money deeper into our pockets and made sure nobody picked them. We were just about to beat a retreat back to our hotel when the two young men returned with the bikes and a pile of cash in a plastic bag, which they handed to us. The business was done – the whole operation took three-quarters of an hour.

(15)

BIKES IN ROMANIA

We glided over town to Bucharest railway station – quite a sizeable, ornamented one in the Central European tradition. The officials were ornamented too, with shabby-smart, red-and-grey uniforms reminiscent of those worn by border guards chasing the Sean Connery Bond over sparsely vegetated hills. For those readers who are familiar with the cosy routines of Eastern European countries of the era, I will not go into too much detail about the tedious and time-consuming procedures mandatory for the obtaining of rail tickets. Suffice it to say that, in such regimes, you do not buy train tickets in the train station, or anywhere remotely near it. Instead, you go across town and enjoy yourself for three and a half hours in Bucharest's state-run (and only) travel bureau where the screeching, milling crowd besieging the counters make a horde of Manchester United lager louts look like a clutch of choirboys at a vicar's tea party.

Starting early, while the kids guarded the bikes back on Platform 1, Jane and I emerged from this melee at noon with tickets for five people and five cycles to Constanza. Fortunately, trains to this coastal town from Bucharest were relatively frequent, so we had chances on the two o'clock, the four o'clock and the seven o'clock trains. We eagerly greeted the first of these transports only to be told, 10 minutes before departure, that they would not take our bikes. This was somewhat of a setback, as we did not have time to check them into left luggage – another alternative. In the two hours remaining before the next train, I went to see the station master. She was a woman – mid-forties, stiff-backed, pudding-faced, bemedalled, bespectacled – an ideological devotee contemptuous of anyone who was not related to Ceauşescu, was not a Hero of the Soviet Union, or who had not accompanied Mao on the Long March. Yes, we had tickets for five bikes to Constanza, but we could not put them on passengers' knees, could we? Passengers' knees in Romania usually had other passengers sitting on them. Yes, there were goods vans on Romanian trains, but they were for priority goods like cabbages, sacks of flour and squawking chickens, not for shiny articles of luxury. There was a left luggage department in the station, but that was for honest suitcases. We couldn't put bikes on shelves, could we? Then what should we do? She looked away in disdain and busied herself saving the regime. She would not even take a bribe, like all the men did. The four o'clock train came and departed, passengers hanging out of the windows.

Things were now getting serious. If we didn't make the seven o'clock, even our lousy passenger tickets would be useless. But what to do with the bikes? At about half past five, after buttonholing everyone who could speak English, French or German, I discovered that there was another stationmaster – one who controlled freight – and that this one was a man. A couple of packets of Kent got me into his office, where he sat chewing gum and doing a crossword under a sizeable portrait of Ceauşescu. He was a small, timid-looking individual, a kind of Balkan Woody Allen.

Still masticating, he motioned me to take a seat. Putting

another pack of Kent on his desk, I poured out my troubles and probably went over the top in intimating what I thought about his bemedalled colleague in the office next door. He seemed to like it and soon started nodding sympathetically. When I had finished my diatribe, he took the chewing gum out of his mouth and addressed me in impeccable English. He had studied for a couple of years in England, was an ardent Arsenal fan and had served four years as the Romanian consul in Tel Aviv. He seemed completely Westernized, obviously relished the opportunity to practise his polished English and chatted away merrily for half an hour, apparently forgetting the dire situation that had brought me to his door. When I dared mention it again, he beamed down his big nose at me, flicked his right hand gaily towards the wall beside him, and assured me that he had already worked out a solution.

'Don't take your bikes to the Black Sea,' he advised. 'They'll steal them for sure!'

'So, what do we do with them?'

'Where are you going after your stay in Romania?'

'Vienna. Then by plane to England.'

'OK. What you do is this: you send your cycles by rail freight to Belgrade. Left luggage does not take bicycles, but our goods department does. I personally will see to it that they leave for Yugoslavia in two or three days' time. They will sit in the goods yard in Belgrade railway station and await your collecting them. You use your rail tickets to Constanza, have your Black Sea holiday, then come back by train to Bucharest and Belgrade. When you've got the bikes, you go by train to Vienna with the cycles in the guard's van. No problem.'

'How do I get the tickets for the bikes?'

'I give them to you now. Five bikes to Belgrade is a pittance.

Don't bother getting a refund for the others – it will take a month.'

Woody was a gem; he didn't smoke, but he accepted a few packets of Wrigley's for future use. Accompanying us to the freight department, he stuck little red 'export' labels on the handlebar of each bike while we attached white ones with 'Lewis, Belgrade' inscribed on them. He shook hands genially with all of us and sent his warmest regards to George Graham, Frank McLintock and Terry Neale. As we clambered aboard the pathetically overcrowded seven o'clock, I mentally said goodbye to our precious Austrian cycles for ever. But a week later at six o'clock in the morning they were waiting for us in a remote, unsupervised siding of Belgrade railway station, tied together with string in the morning mist, with labels intact, unharmed, unpunctured, unguarded and, miraculously, unstolen.

IN DARKEST FINLAND — 1952

Between the fells of Lapland and the inhabited areas in the south lies a great tract of land, vast and melancholy, consisting mainly of trees, lakes, swamps and empty silence. This land, shrouded from the rest of the country by virgin forests and honeycombed by innumerable waterways, is the real heart of Finland. It is the land where thoughts are unhurried, where words are few and where solitude is greatly valued. If we are to believe the stories told of men not speaking to their wives for two years at a time or of trappers knifing would-be neighbours because they dared to build a house within a 5-kilometre radius of their own, thereby intruding upon their privacy, it is here in the dark interior that we shall believe them.

To penetrate this little-known region is no easy task. The road twists and turns like a serpent and often plunges into the lake where rustic ferries have you at their mercy. After a dozen such voyages, however, the countryside takes on that brooding, locked-in look that central Finland has, and you feel that you are getting somewhere. The ferry nightmare will soon put you behind schedule – if you have one – and you will probably wind up spending the night in some small, isolated village which lacks a hotel. That is what happened to us.

During the day we had observed signs telling us we were leaving civilization. Villages had appeared at longer and longer intervals, and the sound of the car had brought mothers rushing out to grab their children and whisk them indoors. In the village where we stopped, the 'No Parking' signs had given way to huge boards nailed on trees bearing the words 'No Tethering Horses Here'. We thought this was rather ominous.

We resolved to make contact with the local inhabitants. Entering the only shop we could find, we asked for today's paper – the day, incidentally, being Wednesday. We were handed Tuesday's paper, which was interesting enough, but we had already read it on Tuesday. We eyed the woman behind the counter.

'Err, we asked for today's paper.'

She gave us a look which might have been suspicion. 'That is today's.'

'But it says here Tuesday.'

'Yes, but it came today.'

'It came today?'

'Yes, and that makes it today's, doesn't it?'

We had to think for a moment. If today's paper was yesterday's, then what we obviously wanted was tomorrow's.

'What about tomorrow's paper?' we ventured bravely.

The look she gave us this time was unmistakeable. But she tried to humour us.

'How can I give you tomorrow's paper when it only comes next Friday?'

We felt rather foolish and went.

It was getting late, and, thinking about bed, we drove up to what was evidently the village hall, in front of which were gathered a couple of dozen people. We broached the subject of our accommodation to a man who wore a tie, and in actual fact he turned out to be the best informed. He was none other than the local detective, and tonight was his big night, since Wednesday was trial night for the criminals of the week, and the building we were in front of was the court. On Mondays it was the theatre, on Tuesdays the cinema, on Thursdays the Municipal Hall, on Fridays the night school, on Saturdays the Youth Club and on Sundays the dance hall. It was the village restaurant and jail at all times.

When we asked him about accommodation, our friend became exasperated in the extreme. Apparently, visitors were regularly granted hospitality in the jail, but that night it was absolutely packed. Beside two murderers, four whisky smugglers and three drunks, they had just caught two fellows stealing horses that very afternoon, and he knew for certain that they were going to get the last two places. He was most apologetic. It was, as he said, a great pity about those two horse-thieves. Otherwise we might have had a jolly old night with the murderers. We looked disappointed, thanked him kindly for his concern, drove on to the next grassy patch beside the road and slept in the car.

The tourist will enjoy this country if he can stand the silence. The people are friendly enough, but they keep to themselves. When, one inky night, a villager called out 'Hi' to a Finn who was in our party and then disappeared into the blackness, we thought he had been fairly expansive. It was only when our friend told us that it was an old university friend of his with whom he had lived for four years and not seen for the last six that we felt we were really beginning to understand these people.

RUSTIC WEDDING

That summer Hägglund and I attended some weddings out in the Finnish countryside. I daresay country weddings anywhere tend to have more colour than city ones, but I always think that a country wedding in Finland has something special about it.

To begin with, there are so many people. They say that all the world loves a wedding, but in Finland you would think that all the world had got in. Attendance is by invitation. In the country, the word 'invitation' has a wide connotation. The recipient is entitled to take along his whole family, servants if he has any, and any other droppers-in, insurance agents and window cleaners who happen to be in the house at the time.

The wedding services take place in the small, white, steep-roofed Lutheran churches that dot the countryside. In church, the numbers are not too great, but this is made up for later. The celebrations are held in village halls, large farmhouses or, in the most picturesque of cases, lofty barns, quaintly decorated for the occasion. There, you have the smell of the hay, the blonde country girls in their colourful costumes, the rows of shuffling red-faced, straw-haired country lads, the spruced-up old peasants with their plain wooden cigarette holders and surreptitious hip flasks, the benign, hawk-eyed minister with his forbidding collar, the gossiping old women, the business-like accordion band, the dazed young couple shaking hands all round, and the harassed father of the bride talking to the village policeman outside the barn door.

Looking back, I have a great nostalgia for those long summer nights when the sun set for only an hour, and even then left the fields illuminated with an unreal, romantic twilight where other young couples flitted quietly from tree to tree and the muted, excited voices carried clearly across the acres. I remember with affection the swirling polkas and jenkkas, the glistening pink cheeks and flashing white teeth, the yellow braids and ponytails, the old men squatting behind their leather countenances and blue cigarette smoke, the serious-faced young woman plucking at her kantele, the sad voice of the folklore singer expressing her attachment to the beautiful, brooding, bleak countryside:

> *Suomessa olen minä syntynyt,*
> *sinisen järven rannalla . . .*

There would be Baltic herrings and boiled new potatoes and hams and chicken and pork to eat, and then generous helpings of sickly-sweet, creamy cake. After the snaps with the herrings, you could drink mead and beer and there was an occasional early *jaloviina* – cut brandy – for the thirsty old men. As the night wore on and the minister retired, there would be less and less eating and more and more drinking, and the dances would take on in colour and rhythm and frenzy. Strange red cheeks would make appearances more frequently at the barn door, the sound of the gaiety and music from the interior would attract the last of the peasants from within the 15-kilometre radius, and there would be a constant coming and going of taxis and hunting for liquor to keep up the rapidly diminishing supply. It was not unusual for the scores of uninvited guests, having eaten their fill, to go scouring the neighbourhood for bottles of spirits and bring them back to the father of the bride. It eased their conscience, besides improving the good man's humour.

Often there were fistfights, and broken noses would spurt red blood over starched white shirts and battered young men would be heard muttering jumbled threats behind dark trees in the forest. Sometimes there would be knife fights, too, and then the consequences would be more serious, but even such events caused considerably less fuss than a non-Finn would expect. All Finnish peasants carry a sheathed *puukko* (a Finnish dagger of finest steel), and Hägglund said that a proper set-to with the knives was all in the good old Finnish country wedding traditions. If you think this is exaggeration, you have never been to a rustic wedding in central Finland.

If you ever go along to one without an invitation, you are advised to reconnoitre in advance and use a little craft at the door. Hägglund is a past master at this practice. One night we turned up outside a barn at about 2am and, by peeping through the cracks, we could see about a hundred people thronging the dance floor and rapidly disposing of all remaining bottles and eatables. The man at the door eyed us suspiciously.

'Some wedding,' said Hägglund by way of introduction.

'Yeah.'

'Plenty of people.'

'Yeah.'

Hägglund offered him a cigarette and lit it for him.

'Some band,' he added presently.

'Not bad.'

'What time did the music start?'

'Dunno.'

'How long have you been here?'

'Half an hour.'

'Weren't you invited?'

'Me? No.'

'Did they let you in all right?'

'Who?'

'Them.'

'Who's "them"?'

'The bride's father and all those invited.'

'Everybody who was invited went home hours ago.'

'But who are all these?'

'No idea.'

'Do you mean to say you don't know who they are?' Hägglund asked sternly.

'No. Who are you?'

It was clear that the man was a fool, so Hägglund pushed him to one side and we went in and finished off the liquor.

The following week, there was another wedding at the village hall, and I told Hägglund that I'd like to try my hand at swindling our way in. We arrived well after midnight, and the first person we saw was a drunk leaning on the doorpost, taking a breather. I decided to pump him first.

'Hello, there,' I said. 'How is it going?'

'Fine,' he replied.

'Plenty to drink?'

'Plenty.'

'Lots to eat?'

'Lots.'

'The minister gone?'

'Yeah.'

'The couple out of the way?'

'Not yet.'

'Ah well, it's all the same – where do we leave our coats?'

'Are you invited?'

'No, but we'll keep out of their way.'

'Out of whose way?'

'The couple's.'

'Oh, I see.'

'She'll think that he invited us.'

'Uh-huh.'

'He'll be so drunk he won't be able to see.'

'Uh-huh.'

'Who's getting married here, anyhow?'

'I AM!'

I don't know why it is that this sort of thing never happens to Hägglund.

THE MARVELLOUS FINNISH POLICE

One evening, I was having dinner at the home of some English friends who live near Winchester. A British executive there, a Mr Robinson, on hearing I had lived in Finland, exclaimed:

'Oh, I love that country – what marvellous policemen!'

This was a new one for me, so I asked him to explain to me and the other guests.

'Well, I was in this little town of Jämsäkoski . . .' he began and proceeded to tell us his anecdote.

He was buying paper from his Finnish colleague, Virtanen. In order to impress the Finns, Robinson had driven to Finland in his new Jaguar, which he parked outside the restaurant where Virtanen had invited him to dinner. At midnight, after a wonderful meal and half a dozen cognacs, Virtanen said goodnight and Robinson had to drive back to his hotel in his Jaguar.

The hotel was on the same street as the restaurant, only 500 metres away. Normally it would have been no problem, but Robinson realized he was very drunk. Should he leave the car in front of the restaurant and walk to his hotel? He thought this would look silly the next morning, so he decided to drive. He drove very slowly, at 5 kilometres per hour. Suddenly, to his horror, he noticed a blue-and-white car, with a sign 'POLIISI', following him.

He felt he could do any of three things: (1) stop, get out and walk; (2) continue to drive to the hotel at 5 kilometres per hour; or (3) speed up and drive normally. He decided that the second option was the safest. The police car followed him at 5 kilometres per hour to the door of the hotel. Robinson got out of the car and made his way up the steps of the hotel entrance. Two policemen got out of the police car and watched him silently. As he opened the hotel door, one of the policemen spoke:

'Good evening, sir!'

'Good evening, Officer!'

'What is your name and what are you doing in Finland?'

'I'm Robinson from Winchester, England, and I'm buying paper from Mr Virtanen.'

'Oh good. One little point, Mr Robinson. Next time you drive along the main street in Jämsäkosi, would you mind putting your car lights on?'

'Oh, thank you, Officer. I certainly will.'

Robinson turned to enter the hotel and then the other policeman spoke:

'Just one more thing, Mr Robinson.'

'Yes?'

'In Finland, we drive on the right. Goodnight, sir.'

Mr Robinson, on the basis of this experience, is a loyal ambassador for Finland as he goes about his business in the UK.

(19)

PUKARO – A SPECIAL PLACE

I have lived rather a long time, and it has been my good fortune to visit well over a hundred countries. From time to time, I have ventured to draw modest comparisons between one place and another and occasionally even dared to pass judgment on someone. Yet I find that the years bring more queries than answers, more doubt than certainty, to my reading of the human mind.

One of the conclusions I have reached, however – and it is now an unshakeable belief – is that some places on this earth are *special*. Special places are relatively few in number (I have come across only two or three on my travels), and it may be that many of us live and die without ever seeing one.

Of course, it all depends on what one means by 'special', and I shall attempt to go into that definition in a moment, but I can tell you that if you have ever been to one of these special places and encountered the type of atmosphere and characters to which I am referring, you will know immediately what I am talking about and you will automatically be an insider or semi-insider to this story.

There seem to be a limited number of places, not particularly isolated geographically, and in developed areas such as England and Scandinavia, which, by virtue of the original or outstanding characteristics of their inhabitants or some freak of local nature, cannot but be regarded as very special both in regard to their own view of the world and their impact on the normal people in surrounding districts. Such places are usually villages of a modest size, with a clannish local population bound together by a strong or incomprehensible dialect. It is questionable if one can ever really understand what produces one of these rare enclaves, or if the circumstances are similar in each case, but it would appear that other basic ingredients are clear-cut borders, a sufficiency of farmers, a supply of local stone or wood to build the village houses, a fair share of poverty, adequate facilities for drinking and brawling, and a general, unswerving acceptance of a score of local superstitions.

In the early 1950s I accepted a job for a year as a farm labourer in the small village of Pukaro in the rural wilds of south-east Finland. I had not been in the job long before I learned that this particular village had a reputation of being undeniably quaint – old-fashioned in its adherence to anachronistic traditions, sturdily independent of others and, above all, famed for a number of violent inhabitants. The most notorious of these was an old worker named Juhani Korhonen, who took care of the horses on the farm (Gammelgård) where I was employed.

Though he was approaching 80, one could tell by the way he handled the horses and wagons that he was still a powerful man; also, it was noticeable that other workers treated him with the utmost deference. There were stories relating to Korhonen's immense strength as a younger man, for he was well over 6 feet and his now slightly stooping posture failed to conceal the undiminished musculature of his broad shoulders. He could still pick up a 40-kilo sack of flour with one hand and swing it into the cart with a flick of the wrist. Feats of his youth had included carrying huge urns full of milk under either arm and dragging barn doors across farmyards. In Finland, they build wooden platforms by the road to take milk urns or other heavy items to await being loaded on to carts. Korhonen had once taken horse and cart to Lapinjärvi to fetch an enormous barrel of cement for the farm. It was of such weight that the two local men destined to place it on the cart were unable to handle it, so, after 10 minutes' rocking and manoeuvring, Korhonen lost patience and asked them to take the reins and back the horse and cart up to him while he took the barrel. Standing on the road, he put his arms round the barrel and, with a loud grunt, swung it round to face the oncoming cart. They handled the horse badly and Korhonen had to hold his barrel for nearly a minute. Finally, they backed the wagon, flap down, under the barrel, which Korhonen gratefully released. The wagon collapsed.

But Korhonen's reputation did not rest on his strength. He had killed three men. In the short time I had known him, I had grown to like him immensely. Silent and withdrawn, with eyes only for what he was engaged in doing, he had a gentle manner which completely belied the roughness of his gnarled, brown hands and craggy features. The horses knew his gentleness, for he treated them like favourite children, softly stroking their mane, jaws and nostrils in moments of rest, feeding them titbits, calming them quietly when they were nervous or overworked. Korhonen paid little attention to me, or to any other human being, but when we sometimes had the occasion to exchange stiff remarks, his very abruptness had a certain understanding and dignity about it. He had had his fill of people, preferring horses and other animals, but one had the feeling that nothing passed him by – his blue eyes were keen, and his thoughts ran deep.

Two of the killings had been accidental, or at least provoked by the victims. In his late forties, he had attended a Finnish country wedding, enjoying to the full the eating, drinking and dancing that took place in the great barn until the early hours of the morning. In a state of some intoxication, he had fallen asleep in the hay and snored happily there for a couple of hours till a drunken farmer woke him up in jest with a *puukko* at his throat. Korhonen was a fast mover in those days and in a flash he had knocked aside the *puukko* at his throat, whipped out his own and sunk it into his attacker's heart.

Under the circumstances, Korhonen was acquitted in court. He and his family moved to a different village, and he continued his life as a farm labourer for a further 10 years. Then, at another wedding, he was taunted and provoked by a very big and very drunken carpenter, who drew his *puukko* and announced Korhonen's imminent departure from this world. He advanced upon Korhonen, who retreated a good 15 metres until a wall at his back obliged him to draw his knife and dispatch his leering tormentor with one lunge through the heart. He is said to have wiped his knife carefully in the hay before putting it back in the sheath and asking his wife to phone up the Lapinjärvi police. He fed the horses before leaving with the police, telling his son how to handle the animals in his absence. He did three years, on account of mitigating circumstances.

When he was in his late sixties, he killed his third Finn, this time in a straight knife fight, but again after being severely provoked. He sustained minor cuts, but again found the heart with unerring accuracy. The message was clear: don't mess around with old Korhonen. He doesn't like violence or knives, but when he does fight, he goes for the kill. A charge of murder was later reduced to manslaughter and Korhonen did five years with a little time off for exemplary behaviour.

Martta Wallen (the owner of the farm) employed him at Gammelgård on the strength of his uncanny ability with horses, and also because she quite liked him. He ceased carrying a *puukko* and kept out of trouble for years. In one of the post-war farm workers' strikes, some pickets tried to stop Korhonen taking the horses to Lapinjärvi for fodder. He explained that he sympathized with them but had to work on certain days to see to the animals' needs. They barred his way on the Monday and the Tuesday, and the horses went without their feed. On the Wednesday, Korhonen again led his animals up to the picket line and asked for free passage, which was refused. Mournfully he took out his *puukko* and asked the pickets which one wanted to die first. When they didn't quite understand, he mumbled something about three or four or five not making an awful lot of difference to him now, at least not at his age. The horses had no feeding problems after that.

Korhonen suffered his final indignity in the winter I was in Pukaro, when he went to a Saturday-night dance in Elimäki, 7 kilometres away, for a quiet drink with his friends. A young Elimäki tough, noted for his violence and bad behaviour, took it upon himself to taunt the ageing Korhonen, whom he depicted as a spent force – a has-been – calling into question Korhonen's legendary reputation. Korhonen ignored him steadily, infuriating the youth by refusing to show any interest in what he was saying. Finally, the ill-advised young man, desperate to establish his superiority, took a beer bottle and cracked Korhonen over the head with it. The old man blinked hard, momentarily stared at the youth, then quietly put on his cap, turned on his heel and made his way out of the waltz-mill. The young tough jeered him all the way to the door and when he had gone, boasted to his friends of his victory. One of the Pukaro labourers addressed the youth, saying:

'Do you know who that is?'

'Of course – feeble old Juhani Korhonen.'

'Do you know where feeble old Juhani Korhonen has gone?'

'Who cares?'

'He's walking the 7 kilometres back to Pukaro to get his *puukko* from his bottom drawer. He will then walk 7 kilometres back here with it. It will take two and a half hours. If I were you, I would not be here when he returns.'

Not only did the youth disappear, but the whole dance hall emptied within the hour, the owner locking it up at midnight. At one o'clock, Korhonen arrived with his *puukko*, tried all the doors and windows in the darkness, saw that all was abandoned, then trudged another 7 kilometres back home to Pukaro.

Korhonen was only one of the unusual characters who inhabited Pukaro. Another was Göran Boije, who dropped in twice a week at Gammelgård, always at mealtimes. The Boijes lived at Lumnäs, the farm adjacent to Gammelgård. They were a noble Finnish family whose records dated back to the twelfth century. Three sisters lived in the manor house, but not Göran. Though of a noble line, he dressed like a tramp and shaved only occasionally. On my third day at Gammelgård, he dropped in for a chat just as the dinner gong sounded. Martta Wallen, who had seen him coming across the fields, already had a place laid, but the usual formalities were observed:

'I was just passing and thought I would drop in for a while.'

Göran would then take his usual place in front of the grand-mother clock. Göran always wore a black jacket with frayed elbows, baggy grey trousers and an 'off-white' shirt, black on the inside of the collar, without tie. He was about 60, sallow of complexion, and wore thick-rimmed spectacles. Peltonen, the foreman, who washed every day, did not approve of him, but Martta and Mathias Wallen found him entertaining, welcoming him unreservedly to their table. He spoke mainly Swedish, in view of his lineage, declaiming all he said in a hoarse, rasping voice, as if he were speaking in church or reading out a list of rules. I found him easy to understand; when he discovered I actually listened to what he said, he would devote at least five minutes of every sermon to me.

He was a classic black sheep: the three Boije sisters had little to do with him. I never saw him at Lumnäs: he lived in a wooden shack about a mile from Gammelgård, in the middle of open farmland. The shack served as a home and a workshop, for Göran actually worked – he had a trade. In spite of his vagabond appearance, he was a skilled metalworker, specializing in wrought iron, though he could hammer brass and copper with the best of them. He would make a variety of articles for the farms of the district – black wrought-iron gates, fancy hinges and doorknobs, metal chandeliers, candlesticks, coffee tables, garden chairs and anything else you could describe for him. Give him a basic idea, he would come back a week later with a drawing and a quotation, and the work would be done some-time in the next six months. You could not rush him. He had an impressive waiting list, stretching all the way from Pukaro to Lovisa. If you wanted a floral-shaped lamp bracket with the name Boije on it, you waited your turn.

Göran was funny about his name. Though he had, in a sense, turned his back on his family and lived the life of a semi-hermit, he never quite let you forget his ancestry. It is said that he once visited Savonlinna Castle, where the coats of arms of all Finland's ancient families are displayed in the Great Hall. He went at an unusual hour and was challenged by an eager young sentry, suspicious of Goran's vile appearance.

'Who are you?' shouted the sentry.

'Who am I?' echoed Göran. 'Listen, young man, I know who I am. The question is, who are you?'

He then is said to have led the boy inside and pointed to the shield bearing the name Göran Boije av Gennäs.

'That, my boy, is who I am,' said our eccentric *Pukarolainen.*

In 1944 Göran was called up in the Finnish Army – an indication of how hard pressed they were. He was sent to a Swedish-speaking regiment at Dragsvik, near Ekenäs (Tammisaari) on the south-west coast. It was not long before the instructors realized that nobody was going to make a soldier out of Göran, who rarely shaved, looked like a tramp in or out of uniform, and pretended not to hear orders or simply ignored them.

Whenever he felt like it, Göran wandered out of the barracks and walked to Ekenäs to buy cigarettes, which he smoked on or off duty. One day, he was returning from such a shopping trip when he was halted at the gate of the garrison by a patrol of military police, who were not from the area and did not know him.

'Why didn't you salute?' shouted the sergeant in charge of the patrol.

'What?' replied Göran vacantly.

'Salute!' screamed the sergeant.

'*Na guda, guda,*' said Göran, which translates roughly as 'Tut, tut'.

The sergeant went up to him, pointed to his MP badge and shouted, 'Do you know what this is?'

The short-sighted Göran suddenly showed some interest, scrutinized the badge an inch away from his nose and replied:

'It's brass, and pretty poor workmanship, too.'

The sergeant blew his top and ordered his men to arrest Göran, but the captain of the guard, seeing what was happening, rushed out and whispered a few words in the sergeant's ear, whereupon Göran sauntered off in his usual reverie.

In the village, there were eccentric and quarrelsome characters of all kinds, with fixed ideas, prejudices and grudges, extraordinary streaks of obstinacy, persecution complexes. Yet I noticed that all these strange peasants had a friendly attitude towards me and my country.

Besides the village drunks, there were rake-like characters such as Malén and Backström, who were men of some substance, but always in trouble. Each with a bit of land, they preferred wheeling and dealing to farming and involved themselves in every kind of peddling from second-hand cars to crayfish. The problem was that as soon as one heard that the other had gone into a new venture, whether trucking or insulated roofing, he had to go into competition at once, so that, as they were roughly equal in resources and intelligence, they invariably ruined each other's business. The fact was that the village was not big enough for the two of them. They would fight regularly – at the *Valssimylly* (the local spot for dancing), in the street, even in other people's houses. Once a month, one would sue the other, though it was never known for one of these cases actually to reach court. One day they set to with knives (for fists and feet could not do justice to their hatred of each other) and Backström came off worst with Malén's *puukko* in his back, right between the shoulder blades. He managed to stagger to

Lotila's store, where he phoned the Lapinjärvi police, saying it was Malén who had killed him. The police jumped in their patrol vehicle and were in Pukaro in 10 minutes. They found Malén and Backström – the latter with his shirt drenched in blood – swigging beer, sympathetically provided by Lotila.

'What about the stabbing?' shouted the police sergeant.

'Oh, that,' replied Backström. 'Just a small misunderstanding.'

'Backström and me are buddies, you know that,' said Malén. 'Nothing happened really.'

And that was all the police got out of them, though the short-tempered sergeant snatched the beer and poured it all over Backström's head.

Then there were the mad Leppänens. Kalevi Leppänen had six children, three of them blond and three brown-haired. The blond ones all behaved typically for children of their age, but the brown-haired ones had more unusual personalities. Paavo was a kleptomaniac, Juha was a recluse who did nothing but fish, while Pirkko talked to trees. Pirkko was the only one we saw much of, as she worked on a nearby farm as a milkmaid. She never talked to the cows and only to people when she had to, but her conversations with trees lasted for hours. In Finland there are lots of trees, and she knew a great number of them. Some days she would talk to the trees near where she worked, but when she had an hour or two to spare, she would chat to Lumnäs trees and Pockar Gård trees and a nice clump of silver birch behind Korhonen's cottage.

She used to say her piece to Gammelgård trees about six or seven in the evening, usually when we were having dinner. That was frequently Pirkko's complaints session, though some-times we would be entertained by a modest sermon or her next day's shopping list. If we were unlucky, she would sing in a cracked, toneless falsetto.

When it got too bad, Martta Wallen, who had taught her at the village school 20 years earlier, would grab the long-handled broom from the porch, run out into the farmyard and brandish it at her. More often than not, Pirkko would go on addressing the trees. When she did return to the house, she would be sure to bid them farewell first.

TEATTERI-GRILLI

At times in life things happen which you would swear are impossible. Such a happening took place one evening in March 1960 in Helsinki. I had just spent a week skiing in Finnish Lapland with Åke Lindman, a well-known actor, Erkki Siirala, the lawyer of Veikkaustoimisto (the Finnish football pools association) and Mrs Hackman, the wife of the owner of Finland's biggest manufacturer of cutlery.

We took the plane from Lapland to Helsinki on Saturday evening, arriving in the capital at 10pm all dressed in our ski outfits and anoraks. Lindman headed off home for an early night – he was due to start a new play the following evening. I was rather tired and was about to depart homewards when Siirala announced that he was taking Mrs Hackman and me for a few drinks. This was always a risky venture with Siirala, as his drinking sessions tended to drag themselves out. He was an overly sociable soul, a bit of a rake, but a good friend, so the two of us concurred. In any case, he was a man not to be denied when he had a plan.

'Where do you think they will let us in in our ski clothes?' asked Mrs Hackman, who knew her way around Helsinki society and was practical by nature.

'We'll go to the Teatteri-Grilli,' replied Siirala.

Mrs Hackman and I had a good laugh as we knew this was

a splendid joke. First, I should describe the restaurant situation in Helsinki in the 1960s. No good restaurant would let a man in unless he wore a suit and no woman could venture in unless she wore a dress. This rule applied any time after 6pm and was rigidly enforced by doormen who could be neither bribed nor turned by other means.

Another feature of restaurant life in the Finnish capital at that time was that most establishments had to close at 11pm or midnight, apart from a privileged few elite ones which could stay open till 1am. The top-class Italian restaurant Monte Carlo had a licence to stay open until 3am; the highly exclusive Teatteri-Grilli had a licence till 4am. Situated just behind the National Theatre, it had a faithful, well-dressed high-society clientele who regularly packed the restaurant from midnight till the hour of four every evening of the week. In any case, you had to book one or two weeks in advance, and for Saturday nights a prior reservation of a couple of months was advisable.

This Saturday night there was a 20-metre queue of immaculately attired would-be diners leading up to the front door, where a thickset attendant admitted couples in the event of others couples leaving. As things were in full swing around 11pm, gaining entry by this manner was painfully slow. Siirala marched up to the front door, his heavy après-ski boots crunching the highly packed powder snow. It was a cold night, and Mrs Hackman and I shivered in his wake (not only because of the temperature). Twenty toffs glared at our effrontery, but nobody bothered to speak, as they knew we would not get in.

Siirala rapped on the door and the doorman opened it a few centimetres to hear him.

'We'd like a table,' said Siirala. The door attendant obviously knew Siirala, so there were no histrionics, but his negative body language indicated that he couldn't let us in.

'Go and fetch Mattila,' said Siirala. Mattila, as everybody in the queue knew, was the assistant manager. Mattila showed up in a few minutes and opened the door about 12 inches. Siirala got his foot in the door.

'We need a table for three.'

Mattila looked over Siirala's shoulder and saw Mrs Hackman and me in our anoraks. (We were also carrying our skis.) The assistant manager laughed nervously and whispered something in Siirala's ear. Siirala laughed in turn, and Mattila's smile turned into an expression halfway between indignation and despair. Mattila kept the door open only a foot and Siirala's boot remained where it was. We heard Siirala say, 'Fetch Karhunen then.' (Karhunen was the manager.)

Karhunen duly arrived after five minutes, and Siirala had a friendly chat with him. It was not short conversation, but it was not too long, either. Siirala had begun pointing to a table quite near the (glass) door occupied by a smart couple. The young woman was blonde and pretty; her burly partner was Ingemar Johansson, a Swedish boxer, then the Heavyweight Champion of the World. The Swede seemed none too pleased at the sight of Siirala pointing at his table, though, as a well-known public figure, he was used to more than casual attention. He was even less pleased when Karhunen asked him and his lady to move to a smaller table which magically appeared a few yards away, near the wall. Though less than delighted, the pugilist and his escort eventually did the right thing, and five minutes later Siirala was sitting in his chair as the waiter hastily rustled up an extra chair so that Mrs Hackman and I could be accommodated.

After a change of tablecloth and our anoraks and skis being whisked away to a dark corner of the establishment, the three of us enjoyed three hours' dining and drinking under the hostile gaze of not only the shivering queue outside but also that of the properly attired diners who surrounded us. I never dared look back at Ingemar Johansson, though Mrs Hackman sneaked a few peeps in his direction. Siirala ignored him from start to finish. When we left at 2.30 a few remaining stragglers were quickly admitted by the nervy doorman who managed a quick nod of acknowledgment to Siirala as the latter hailed a taxi.

Mrs Hackman and I related this incident many times to our friends over the next couple of years. Nobody ever believed us, so eventually we gave up telling it. I lost contact with Siirala, as I went off to Japan for a few years, but around 1980 I bumped into him in Tenerife. I was on holiday; he had retired to the Canaries. We greeted each other warmly and had a few drinks and a couple of dinners together. On the second evening, I could not contain my curiosity any longer.

'Erkki,' I said, 'do you remember the night 20 years ago when you got three of us into the Teatteri-Grilli on a Saturday night wearing ski clothes?'

He did.

'Erkki, for God's sake, how did you do it? We are both getting older, one of us might die and then I'll never know.'

He drank another double whisky before he replied.

'Do you know how the Teatteri-Grilli got its licence, year after year, to stay open until four o'clock?'

'No.'

'The licence, renewable every year, was granted annually by the Helsinki Nightwatchman Committee – an august body if ever there was one.'

'And?'

'From 1955 to 1965 I was the chairman of that committee.'

DONKEYS IN ST THOMAS

Sailing the Caribbean, we put in at St Thomas, one of the larger of the Virgin Islands. After a month visiting such islands as St Lucia, St Vincent, Grenada and Virgin Gorda, I had got used to the delightful calypso lilt of Caribbean English, which varies only slightly all the way from Jamaica to Trinidad.

Walking into town from the harbour, I fell into the company of a black policeman. We chatted about this and that as we walked.

'You have no Caribbean accent,' I told him.

'I don't play cricket either – I'm not from the Caribbean. We have black people in the United States, too. I'm American.'

'Where from?'

'Harlem.'

Now I recognized his accent.

'So, this is the United States.'

'Right. You are in the American Virgins.'

'I wasn't sure' I said, 'we just blew in.'

'Welcome to St Thomas!' He was a friendly cop – young and full of energy.

'I wasn't sure,' I repeated, 'because the traffic is driving on the left, just like in Antigua and the British Virgins.'

'That's right, goddammit, we drive on the left.'

'But in other American islands, you drive on the right.'

'That's correct.'

'Then why here on the left?'

'That's a good question, friend. That means I don't know the answer.'

Further on, we met an old man, also black, but speaking Caribbean English.

'Hey, Viv, we got a question for you,' said my policeman friend.

'What's that?'

'Why does St Thomas drive on the left when it's American?'

'It's all to do with them donkey carts.'

'Donkey carts?'

'In old times we always drove on the left, just like the rest of the English-speaking Caribbean.'

'And then?'

'When the US took over, they said we had to drive on the right, and one day they switched – just like that.'

'And why did they change back?'

'It was them donkeys. All the cars and trucks drove on the right, but you know that most of the traffic here 20 years ago was donkey carts.'

'Well, didn't they obey the law like everybody else?'

'Sure they did. But most of these carts were running in rural areas and sometimes doing long stretches, so that the donkey drivers often fell asleep in the noonday sun.'

'And then?'

'When they fell asleep, the donkeys went back over to the left, like they was used to.'

'But didn't that cause a lot of accidents?'

'Hundreds in the first two months, so the government switched everybody back to drive on the left.'

'Couldn't they train the drivers?'

'Sure, training them to obey the law was no problem. But they couldn't train the donkeys.'

RAIN IN AGRIGENTO

Italians and Finns quite like each other; in fact in my opinion, they are attracted to each other as opposite poles are supposed to be. There is no doubt that Finnish men find Italian women glamorous, Italian men find Finnish blondes seductive, and the women of each country have no problems relating to each other. Finnish males and Italian males are another matter: while their different lifestyles and background are of considerable interest, their communication styles do not gel.

It is largely a question of 'to say it or not to say it'. In Finland it is generally accepted that one says only that which is necessary to say. The main function of speech is to give and receive information. Finns do not need to be told anything twice, if they heard it the first time. If they know your name is Bill, they don't say things like 'Listen, Bill' or 'Look at that, Bill.' If they are obviously talking to you, the use of your name is superfluous. When talking to Americans, they are irritated by phrases, such as 'Look here, Paavo' or 'I'll tell you what, Paavo.' Finnish women are less taciturn than the men but even they dislike saying things twice. My friend Michael Gates, who lives in Finland, phoned an HR officer with whom he had business and asked how she was. 'I'm fine,' she replied cheerfully. The following week he needed to speak to her again and rang her up once more.

'How are you, Riitta?' he asked. 'You asked me that last week' was her reply.

On another occasion Michael tried to sell a course of lessons to Eero Soininen, who represented a paper and pulp company.

'We can let you have these lessons at a unit price of 50 euros,' offered Michael.

Eero remained pensive, said nothing. Michael let a couple of minutes pass, then said:

'Well, for you, Eero, we'll make a special price of 48 euros.'

Soininen remained silent, and seemed a little worried. Michael sensed he might lose the sale. He commented on the good quality of the teaching for a couple of minutes, and Soininen nodded but remained clammed up.

Michael finally gave in: 'Eero, my final offer: 45 euros. In all conscience I can't go any lower than that.'

Soininen said, 'I accept.'

Michael heaved a sigh of relief. A reasonable sale was better than no sale.

A month later, he was having coffee with Soininen and congratulated him on his negotiating technique.

'You're a wily old bird, Eero, the way you brought me down to 45 euros.'

Soininen shrugged and replied:

'Actually, I was quite happy with 50 euros. I wanted to say I was satisfied but didn't know the preposition. Was it satisfied with your offer or about your offer or at your offer? While I was trying to decide, you came down to 45.'

A friend of mine, Raimo Jokinen, is an accountant by profession and a particularly taciturn Finn. He wouldn't tell you what day it was if he thought you had a diary in your pocket. At a Helsinki party, I introduced him to Dr Francesco Ingrassia, a banker from the Bank of Sicily – an even closer friend of mine. Raimo was interested in the Bank of Sicily's operations and the two had a couple of reasonable conversations, discussing banking and accounting.

Italians are by nature loquacious; in Italy words are cheap. Italians will use 10,000 words to describe a proposal or an event about which they think you should be properly informed. Finnish males, who use about 10,000 words in a lifetime, tend to drown in Italian loquacity. They just cannot digest it all and consequently get irritated.

Francesco was Sicilian to the core, and therefore more talkative than the average Italian. Raimo's tolerance of him diminished at every meeting. They remained on speaking terms, however. When Raimo planned a holiday in Italy, Francesco insisted he visit Sicily, where he, Francesco, would be the perfect guide. Raimo resisted this suggestion for many months, suspecting he might be in for an overdose of Francesco's kind attentions. However, in July the three of us found ourselves strolling among the famous ruins of Agrigento on the west coast of Sicily. The ruins are superb – vast, majestic, admirably preserved – and Francesco was at his articulate best. Then, suddenly it began to rain.

'Raimo, Raimo!' exclaimed Francesco. Raimo grunted. 'Raimo, it's raining! Can you imagine, it's raining!'

'I don't need to imagine. I can see that it is raining.'

'But this is July!'

'Francesco, I know it is July. Believe me, I know.'

'But this is Agrigento!'

'Oh, it's Agrigento, is it? Well, I knew we were not in Helsinki.'

'But, Raimo, IT IS RAINING IN JULY IN AGRIGENTO!'

'Francesco, I can see for myself that it is raining, we have been in Agrigento for two hours, so I know we are here, and it has been July now for 10 days. Will you please stop telling me about it.'

I felt sorry for Francesco, the kindest of men. It stopped raining 10 minutes later, but Francesco did not dare mention it.

23

LEFT IN OXFORD

They say you never learn from the lessons of life, and that is how it must be with me. The year after our English course in Bangor, we held another one at Bishop Otter College in Chichester. This time only Finns and Italians – no Japanese. As usual, the Finns were dutiful students, spoke only English with each other and, apart from a few cases of inebriation in the bar between eleven and midnight, posed no problems at all. The Italians – 28 of them – were quite a handful, what with their persistent tardiness, volubility, appetite for jesting (one time they tolled the college fire bell at midnight) and general uncontrollability. They were, however, a lovable lot, and we did our best to make them enjoy their stay. In classes they combined well with the Finns; we were careful not to organize any major joint excursions.

One exception was trips to Oxford. As the university city was only 80 kilometres from Chichester, the Italians decided en bloc that they wished Oxford to be their Wednesday-afternoon excursion, not only the first week, but every week. We had no objections; also five Finns said they would like the same arrangement. As we had a 39-seater bus, everybody fitted in nicely.

As I was rather busy organizing lessons, I looked around for someone to whom I could delegate matters of transport. As it happened, one of the Finns, Martti Karttunen (45 years old), was a personal friend of mine and was in the travel business back home. He was noted for his powers of organization and unflappability. He kindly agreed to supervise the Oxford excursions leaving every Wednesday immediately after lunch and returning to Chichester for dinner at 7.30pm.

The first Wednesday Martti left with five Finns and 23 Italians. He was a bit nervous once there as the Italians immediately split up into small groups and rambled all over the city. However, at 6.30 he collected everybody and got back to Chichester with five Finns and 21 Italians. He had been assured on leaving that the party was complete. Two irate Italians had been left stranded in Oxford and had to be brought back (expensively) by taxi.

On the second Wednesday, Martti counted everybody carefully as they boarded the bus in Chichester: five Finns and 20 Italians. He turned his back for a moment and missed two Italians who scrambled in late. In the evening he returned with five Finns and 20 Italians instead of 22. More irate phone calls, another taxi.

On the third Wednesday he counted five Finns and 18 Italians getting on the bus. He double-counted them once they were seated, then ordered the driver to leave at once. In the evening he returned with a more worried look than usual: he brought back five Finns and 21 Italians instead of 18. Half an hour later we had the usual phone call from Oxford announcing five Italians had been left behind. Two taxis were needed this time.

The mathematics were, of course, impossible, but the Italians had defeated us again. Unknown to Martti, eight Italians had gone to Oxford mid-morning under their own steam, then, seeing our bus in its usual place at 6.30, had jumped aboard for a free ride back. As Martti found it hard to distinguish one Italian from another, he had sanctioned departure.

After that we put Martti in charge of the German bird-watching group, and he was untroubled for the rest of the summer.

THE SCIENTISTS

Uffe studied chemistry. He was a serious student and he got a good degree. He was a very quiet boy. He was from Finland.

After he qualified, he got married and emigrated to Canada. There he worked in industry and had five children in eight years. He built a big, wooden house for them all to live in, but found it difficult to study because of the noise.

When the youngest was two, Uffe started going down to the university three or four evenings a week and did research in the laboratory. He knew another chemist, a German named Oscar, whom he could not stand as a person but liked as a chemist. They did research together.

After a while, they began to publish papers in the chemists' journals, and they established something of a reputation in their field. It was a very narrow field, but all research is highly specialized today. They were studying lymph in lower forms of sea life. They published their discoveries in the journals. They had controversies with other chemists in Thailand and Japan. The university let them have a lab on their own. Uffe's mother wrote and said she had always known Uffe would do something like that.

I used to play chess with him on the nights he wasn't in the lab. He was a good player, but very absent-minded. When he took an hour over a move, you knew either he was planning a clever one or he had forgotten he was playing chess.

We played at his place after the children had gone to bed. If I didn't leave when the clock struck 12, Uffe would get to his feet and say he would have to be going home.

One night I accompanied Uffe to the university to watch him and Oscar at work. How many of us would like to see scientists in action? The thrill of discovery; the interplay of brilliant minds; the far-reaching decisions. I was curious and eager to witness the scene.

Oscar was sitting near a jungle of test tubes, retorts, rubber tubing and Bunsen burners. He was looking at the ceiling and ignored our entry. The jungle bubbled quietly.

Uffe went into a glass office in the corner of the lab and put on a white coat. He sat on the edge of a wooden chair and stared out of the window over the lawns. He had a faraway look in his eyes, like Oscar. I took a seat near him and tried to read some of the journals.

He stared out of the window for two hours. The second hour he had his mouth open.

Suddenly Oscar jumped up, ran into the glass office and sat down next to Uffe. They both stared at the lawns for half an hour and then Oscar said:

'It was the square root.'

Uffe turned his head and threw him a look of intense suffering. Oscar bit his lip and nodded a dozen or so times.

They kept this up for 10 minutes. Uffe sighed and looked out of the window again: 'Yes.'

Oscar went out and stood in the middle of the lab, staring at the floor.

Uffe stuck his hand out sideways, and I lit a cigarette and passed it to him. He smoked spasmodically and the ash dropped at his feet.

Oscar came in again and tapped Uffe on the shoulder.

'Uffe.'

Uffe glanced up, startled.

'Uffe.'

'What?'

'Why did I go out?'

'Out?' Uffe had a baffled look.

'What was it I went out for?'

'Did you go out?'

Oscar sat down once more, and they stared at the lawns while I read another journal.

One of the retorts cracked and all the liquid ran out. There was a loud crash and half the jungle fell over. Neither of them heard it.

When I told them, they scampered like rabbits and picked pieces of glass up from the floor and wrung their hands in anguish.

As I helped them to clean it up, I thought how much faster their progress would be if I were there to organize for them a bit and I laughed aloud.

They both stared at me as if I were mad.

We are all in their hands.

NORTH KOREA – THE CLOSED COUNTRY

In North Korea, Westerners experience encounters of a striking cross-cultural nature every day. I give only a few examples in the following pages.

At various times in recorded human history, some countries have been closed to outsiders, often for quite long periods. The most significant example in recent times is perhaps the isolation of Japan from 1600 to 1853, initiated and enforced by the Tokugawa dynasty. This self-imposed quarantine led to the Japanese developing a singular, almost unique type of society whose disciplined, collective and moralistic behaviour is without parallel in the modern era.

Since the Second World War, access to certain states has been restricted, in varying degrees, to visitors from the West. Burma/Myanmar, Cuba, Vietnam, large areas in Siberia and China come into this category. There is no doubt, however, that in the post-war period the hardest nation to penetrate has been North Korea.

In 1979 an opportunity came up to enter the Korean People's Republic. The World Table Tennis Championships were scheduled to be held that year in Pyongyang. The North Koreans, though reluctant to open their borders, could not hold the event without letting in the world's table tennis players, their managers, coaches and – horror of horrors – Western journalists. That is how I suddenly became assistant coach to the Finnish table tennis team, just as Ian Wooldridge simultaneously became the table tennis correspondent of the *Daily Mail*. My Finnish friends were only too delighted to join in this mild conspiracy, and various other British and Western European individuals who had never seen a table tennis ball smashed in anger in their entire lives penetrated Kim Il-sung's steely borders under the guise of similar subterfuges.

Getting inside the country is one thing. Moving around and seeing what you want to see is another. We were guests in their country, but it was not left to our imagination to see that we were unwanted, decadent, only temporarily tolerated guests. You will be supervised (you could say chaperoned) by a team of guides, interpreters and minders. In North Korea you are never lonely, except in your inner being. The minders mind, from 8am to your chosen bedtime, with a dedication and thoroughness rarely displayed by 'workers' in the West. They were not easily shaken off. They had the last drink with you in the bar at night. They hung around the lobby an extra half hour after you retired, just in case you changed your mind about sleeping or attempted to sally forth unminded. It was dangerous to do that, they said. There was much hatred around. People might think you were American and duff you up, even maim or accidentally kill you. But what about the American table tennis players? The minders frowned. Well, they had special bodyguards to protect them, was their eventual reply.

It was just as bad in the morning, for they waited for you, sunk deep in the red velvet armchairs of the hotel lobby. I used to run every day before breakfast, but my male minder was there at 7.30 and stopped me. Then they gave me a younger male minder who let me run but ran with me. They were boring runs, I can tell you, past all Kim Il-sung's most imposing edifices (commentary provided). I was finally able to defeat this system by running out of the lobby at 6am, when I discovered that even the most assiduous minder was not able, or willing, to make it before 6.30. There are limits to human devotion, I found, even to the Beloved Leader.

On the morning following our arrival, I was re-interviewed by a more senior official who informed me that I, as an official-cum-educated tourist, would enjoy several additional privileges. He handed me a form to fill in which asked me to request what aspects of Korean life I wished to familiarize myself with. There was a suggested list, which included visits to factories, power stations, dams, farms, universities and so on. I filled the form in eagerly, requesting visits to a school, a university, a farm, a Korean family at home. The official politely added the Museum of the Revolution, the Museum of Korean National History, the Children's Palace and the birthplace of Kim Il-sung at Mangyongdae.

The Koreans were as good as their word in terms of complying with these requests. I never managed to see a university, but the rest I got. Of course, there was a price to pay – everything was meticulously stage-managed – but these forays about town and across the countryside allowed one insights into the actual state of affairs in North Korea that could never have been gained sitting in a stadium. Our minders pounded our ears with propaganda on all these outings – a political doctrine and string of incredible assertions which made Russian or Chinese dogma relatively modest and liberal by comparison – but nevertheless they could not deny us our eyes to see, our judgment to discern, our stomachs to rumble.

Let us take our visit to a Korean school. We were driven 15 kilometres out of town to a suspiciously new-looking building which housed a dozen classrooms filled with a couple of hundred of the cleanest kids that I have ever seen. Their faces were a well-scrubbed reddish-brown, their eyes – which never left us – bright but glazed at the same time (if you can imagine that). They were dressed in neatly pressed uniforms, sat upright at tiny wooden desks and chanted periodically in uncanny unison whenever teacher gave subtle signals. They were about 10 years old, the teacher about 70. After witnessing some art classes, where the children showed considerable talent and dexterity, we were treated to a music class where an eight-year-old Rubinstein gave an impeccable rendering of one of Chopin's Preludes, followed by the whole class singing a few stirring songs dedicated to the Beloved Leader.

The headmistress, perhaps in an unguarded moment, had let it slip that the school taught English from the age of 12 – so I asked to see an English class in progress. This was clearly not in the script, and my minder was tic-tacking full-time behind my back, but eventually, with some un-Asian insistence, I was able to corner them into letting me enter the English class. This was allowed only after some five minutes' frantic preparation, which resulted in the entire class chanting 'Good morning, dear Visitor,' as I entered the room. I suppose I stayed about 10 minutes, walking round the classroom and inspecting an assort-ment of English pieces pinned to the walls; they were strictly revolutionary – anti-American songs and quotations from the Beloved Leader – but at any rate they had got the language right. It was the only English around; nobody spoke any.

I asked the teacher, a young man in his mid-thirties, where he had learned his English. I might as well have addressed him in Martian. He tittered nervously and kept switching his head between me and my minder till I thought he would swoon out of dizziness. I talked to the children too, but apparently they had not quite reached that particular lesson. 'What is your name?' proved exceptionally difficult for them, though one bold youngster did say 'yes'.

Kim, my minder-cum-fellow-jogger, was fairly ratty with me for the rest of the day but had recovered some Asiatic composure when, on the following morning, I was taken to see 'the typical Korean family at home'. Again, it was a (seemingly mandatory) 15-kilometre drive out of town, before we came upon a very small development of a dozen or so flats – white, compact, brand new or newly painted – with a smiling 'caretaker' to greet us and show us round. I was somewhat surprised that North Korean janitors looking after modest apartment blocks in a remote suburb of West Pyongyang should be equipped with flawless English, but we took what we could get.

Since our arrival in the country, we had been told repeatedly that every family in North Korea enjoyed the amenities of a three-bedroom flat (unlike the 10-in-a-room situation in the smelly slums of South Korea). We were indeed shown into a small but satisfactory sitting room to meet Mr and Mrs Sam – the prototypical Korean family with their two kids aged around four and six. This nuclear family, well dressed and smiling, shook hands with us somewhat awkwardly and then stood to attention while Kim described the flat. We saw the kitchenette and toilet and bedrooms one, two and three. Kim counted them on his fingers. Mr Sam, dressed up for the occasion, spoke a little English until I asked him what his job was and whether he had taken a day off work. After some discussion with Kim in Korean, it appeared he was an engineer. The director of his factory had given him a couple of hours off to meet important foreign tourists. He would work overtime that evening so as not to disrupt production.

The bedrooms had beds, but no bedside tables, lamps or cupboards. In the sitting room there was nowhere to sit. The kitchen cupboards, which I naughtily opened, were bare. Kim, who had some difficulty in restraining himself from spanking the back of my hand, explained that the Sams were just moving in. The state was about to transfer their belongings from the three-bedroom apartment which they had previously enjoyed. Perhaps that was why there were no bulbs in the hanging sockets, I said. Everybody agreed, the Sam couple in sign language.

The next day we visited a farm. It was a farm unlike any other I have ever seen. It was a farm without animals, crops, workers or even fields. But it did have a shop, in the middle of nowhere, selling the farm's produce. The shop had no customers, but there were five cheerful saleswomen in starched white aprons and Beloved Leader badges. The shelves of the shop were stacked with tins, not just here and there, but along their entire length.

The number of unsold tins matched to a centimetre the measurements of the shelves. I asked Kim how often they did inventories but was not able to get across the concept. On request, one of the young women put six of the tins on the shiny counter in front of me. I could not read the labels, but coloured images suggested tinned meat, fish (sardines?), corn and an asparagus-like vegetable. It was a very successful farm, said Kim.

'Where are the fields and the workers?' I asked.

'Over there,' replied Kim, pointing vaguely to a blue haze in the north, away from Pyongyang. I tried to buy my six tins, but it was not appropriate, said Kim. Everything by quota, you understand.

AN EXCURSION

My next outing, however, gave me a much clearer picture of North Korean farming. On the first Friday after our arrival in North Korea we were scheduled to make the excursion to Kumgangsan where we would climb the mountain. For some reason the only people to volunteer for this excursion, apart from myself, were seven officials of the French contingent. We were assigned to a Russian minibus, which we shared with a driver and three minders – two male and one female. The young woman, who spoke reasonable French, was interpreter-guide. My friend Kim was left behind. We left at 5am and drove across the peninsula to the port of Wonsan where we stopped for breakfast. The route then took us along the east coast of North Korea, heading south into the mountainous region. Rattling along the coast road, we were not more than 30 metres from the sea. Between the road and the sandy shore there were two parallel fences, about 2 metres apart. They were 3 metres high and clearly electrified. There was no break in this barrier, apart from gates at regular intervals. The gates were manned by armed guards.

My companions, being French, were considerably less inhibited than I was in the realm of asking awkward questions and making sceptical comments. I suppose I had lived in Japan too long to be able to match the biting satire of a Parisian who has been eating Korean food for a week. What was the fence for?

For safety, replied the poor interpreter. Whose safety? The safety of the people. Safety from what – crocodiles? Sorry, why do you speak of crocodiles? Who is the fence meant to keep out? South Korean fascist pig invaders. When are they coming? They could arrive any day. We must be prepared to repel the invasion of the fascist pigs. You don't think the fence is there to stop your people leaving the country? Of course not, we live in paradise. Where did you learn your French? At university. Have you ever been to France? No. Wouldn't you like to visit Paris? I would go there if requested to do so by our Leader. Wouldn't you like a holiday in France? I have my duty here.

The French gave the interpreter-guide a hard time all the way down the east coast. The two male trusties were hamstrung as they didn't speak French. From time to time they interrogated the hapless woman in guttural Korean, occasionally shouting at her out of sheer frustration. The French laughed, jeered and sneered openly; I thought we were all going to wind up in a Korean clink. My own behaviour was so gentlemanly by comparison that the minders ignored me, and I was able to sneak a couple of pictures of the electrified fence.

Later in the morning, as the road took us inland, we suffered a puncture. This turned out to be an incredible piece of luck, as it happened adjacent to a large open area of rice paddies in which laboured scores of peasants. We poured out of the bus like cons in a jailbreak and spread across a few fields before the trusties could stop us. Most of the peasants stopped working and gaped at us in sheer amazement. The French bombarded them with Parisian argot and offered everybody Gauloises; the interpreter scuttled from one to the other like a hen marshalling wayward chicks. One trusty helped the driver change the wheel with a rusty old Russian jack. The other stuck to me like glue as I tried, in vain, to make conversation with a young labourer. The man I had selected to talk to did not look at all like a peasant, and I pointed this out to my minder. He spouted out the explanation proudly. The labourer concerned was a bank clerk who gave his services free of charge to the Beloved Leader every Friday, helping Korean agriculture recover from the previous year's drought. All office workers did this, he boasted. You too? Of course, when I am not engaged in matters of national importance.

It was now clear to me why all office workers in Pyongyang had faces burned by the sun and why, that Friday morning, we had seen dozens of lorry-loads of people being driven into the countryside at 6am. I told my trusty I was moved by this proof of loyal patriotism. He thanked me, dewy-eyed. I was really scoring points against the French that day.

Then suddenly we witnessed something very (North) Korean. As we surveyed the rice-planting, we were vaguely aware of some music in the distance. This now grew louder; we turned our heads to seek out the source. On the road adjacent to the rice paddies, and approaching our stricken bus, came pedalling a female cyclist in a red blouse and flowing black skirt. She seemed to find the cycling laborious and no wonder, for the pedalling powered a loudspeaker attached to the back mudguard, just as a dynamo provides power to a bike headlamp. Revolutionary songs blared out from the speaker, over the fields, where the peasants and their part-time colleagues bent their backs. 'Victory is ours under your guidance, dear Beloved Leader' was the introduction, and ending, to each piece. If the woman had the wind against her, or if she tired at intervals, the music slurred. If she was assisted by a stiff breeze, the rhythm picked up again. What a job, I thought – hard work, low pay, no applause. I was wrong; my Gallic friends lined her path, clapped, cheered, shouted in sheer Latin exuberance. Eyes fixed on the road, she ignored them entirely – just pushed on along her allotted stretch. She was doing her bit.

We reached the foot of Kumgangsan about noon. After an indifferent snack – the French had contrived to bring their own sandwiches, which they shared with me – we began the four-hour climb. It was a perfect spring day, cool, sunny, the sky azure and cloudless. It is hard to imagine a more beautiful mountain. The highest peak in a mountain range stretching for 50 kilometres, Kumgangsan rivals Yosemite National Park in the variety and luxuriance of its scenery. As we climbed, we brushed through colourful shrubs and ferns of many species; majestic cedars, cypresses, maples, chestnuts and sycamores, as well as conifers of all kinds that afforded us welcome shade and splashes of colour. Half a dozen exquisite waterfalls punctuated our route, one of them more than 100 metres high; soaring chimneys and dark spinneys surrounded the summit, where rocky crags enabled us to squat and contemplate a breath-taking panorama. The range stretched endlessly inland, disappearing in a dark blue haze on the western horizon. The afternoon sun filtered through a myriad of leaves and foliage, allowing the keen photographers among us a rich harvest of subjects.

On such a climb, arduous, but in no way risky, the excitement of the ascent, the welcome physical exercise and exertion, the stunning loveliness of the environment, the common innocent goal, bonded the French, the minders, the interpreter and myself in the most comforting manner. One gave one's hand to another across swirling streams, helped the older members up the more difficult spinneys, shared the chores of leading, carrying and picture-taking. For four hours we were all friends suspended in time in a real paradise where dogma, revolutions, victories and defeats, Beloved Leaders, presidents and monarchs held no sway, where the only ideology was one of the moment – the reaching of the summit which would bequeath us an incomparable vision of nature and the quintessential landscape of the Land of the Morning Calm.

How nice this land could be, I thought, as we rested at the top and drank in the spectacle. They have it all right here. The minders smiled at me, aware of my delight in the environment. The interpreter suddenly looked approachable.

The congeniality of this *entente cordiale* dissipated fast as we descended. The French, who became increasingly peckish, talked incessantly of *bifteck avec pommes frites*, a topic which reminded my stomach to churn and lessened some of my own cordiality towards our Korean hosts. The long trip back along the same route afforded us numerous glimpses of toiling bank clerks, post office employees and shop assistants doing their Friday diligence until darkness engulfed us. The lorry-loads of weary volunteers accompanied us along the highways as they returned to Pyongyang and other towns along the way.

PANMUNJOM

If one thing stands out in my memory more than anything else about my visit to North Korea, it is the trip we made to Panmunjom. This was one of the optional excursions offered to educated tourists. I had urged Ron Crayden, one of the senior British officials (who had also received a special classification), to take advantage of this opportunity to witness a real piece of history. He took my advice and came with me; we were the only two foreigners to do this.

At the end of the bitterly fought Korean War in 1952, the American generals Matthew Ridgway and Mark W. Clark concluded and signed an armistice on the mutually agreed frontier between North and South Korea. The armistice was followed by 'peace talks' aimed at stabilizing and normalizing relations between the two Koreas, at establishing a no-man's-land 500 metres wide between the two territories, and ultimately at working towards an eventual reunification of the country through the electoral process. This last objective was hardly considered to be attainable in the foreseeable future, and the talks soon developed into vicious bickering sessions where each side accused the other of violations of the armistice terms. These regular meetings, now numbering in high hundreds, took place in a long dismal Nissen hut in no-man's-land slap on the frontier in the previously undistinguished village of Panmunjom. Grim-faced delegations from North and South Korea (with US participation) face each other at regular intervals on opposite sides of long, narrow, green-baize-covered tables. At the end of the room stands a leather-topped desk where Clark signed the historic document. The meetings are not for the faint-hearted. Hostile in the extreme, they have been noted for their irascibility, petulance, vindictiveness and pugnacity. In 58 years, the progress towards any form of amity or entente has been virtually nil. Two American officers who foolishly went crawling round in the barbed wire of no-man's-land were seen, attacked and hacked to pieces by North Korean guards armed with hatchets. The pieces were returned to the South Korean side in brown sacks.

We could hardly believe that we were going to be allowed to 'inspect' this notoriously dangerous boundary, and we could not conceive what form this exercise would take. We were in for a lesson in North Korean stage management. The 150-kilometre journey to the frontier took three hours. Ron Crayden and I were accompanied by an older minder whom neither of us had seen before. His English was excellent, but he was unsmiling and seemed to brood a lot. It was Friday again, and Ron and I waved at lorry-loads of bank clerks off to their weekly rice business. They ignored us; by contrast, groups of school children at the wayside cheered our car vociferously. (They have been told to cheer all cars. All cars are government cars.)

In the neighbourhood of Panmunjom we were shown some Stone Age monuments. They were impressive, and we took some nice pictures. Later we were taken to a giant statue of Kim Il-sung, situated on a green hill overlooking, at a distance of less than 1 kilometre, the undulating fields of South Korea. It is an impressive statue. It is the third biggest in the world after that of *The Motherland Calls* in Volgograd (formerly Stalingrad) and the Statue of Liberty in New York. Kim, in black marble, surveys with bulging eyes the territory which he has vowed he will reincorporate into the homeland. South Koreans can see the statue from miles off. It is so big, you almost have to back off into South Korea to get it all into your viewfinder when taking a picture.

We, of course, had our ears pounded for some time as we gravitated round the sculpture, but after that we were taken to a house where we sat in red-velvet armchairs for four hours without much to do or any intelligent conversation. Apparently, there had been a hitch in the arrangements, and it was no longer sure that we should be allowed to see the frontier. The spring sun threatened to set, and the shadows of some nearby poplars began to lengthen. When the evening light was really nice and mellow and we had given up hope, we were summarily and peremptorily whisked off to the frontier post. This proved to be a fine marble and concrete building, about 40 metres long, aligned along the North Korean side of no-man's-land. Once inside, Ron and I were introduced to six military personnel – a colonel, a captain and four privates. The privates formed a square around us, the colonel led from the front and the captain stood behind us. We were marched off to a well-furnished waiting room where we were served tea. We were then subjected to 45 minutes' indoctrination by the captain, who was competent in well-versed, rhetorical English. He described the events of the 1950–52 Korean War, from the North Korean perspective, of course. He then asked Ron and myself a series of questions, which required 'yes' or 'no' answers. It was cleverly done, as soon one found oneself endorsing the North Korean position:

'In this internal Korean dispute, were the South Koreans the ones who first called in foreign interventionists?'

'Yes.'

'Did Japan, supposedly neutral, allow the United States to use their country as a supply base against the North Koreans?'

'Yes.'

'Did the Japanese supply the American army with materiel for the duration of the war?'

'Yes.'

'Did Japan make a lot of money out of the Korean War?'

'Yes.'

'Did North Korea accept any outside help until the Americans bombed the Yalu River frontier with China?'

'No.'

I cannot remember all the questions – they did not allow us to take notes – but there were many much cleverer and more subtle than the ones I can recall. I found myself saying all kinds of things I didn't mean. Poor Ron sounded like Karl Marx. After a while I played the game according to their rules and feigned some sympathy for the North Korean cause. The captain was not stupid, yet I detected a gleam of interest in his eyes.

When I had used the term 'Leader' a couple of times (I could not bring myself to say 'Beloved'), his solidarity quickened. His reasoning, previously pompous, became more empirical and appealing. He suspected I might be on his side. He was wrong, but even Wiganers can flatter to deceive. Ron joined in a bit, too. The captain snapped orders to the privates, and we were all on our feet. The colonel, mute all the while, took up his vanguard position and led us off on the double down a short corridor. We had to march in rhythm with the six of them – all in full red-trimmed khaki uniforms, of course. At the end of the corridor it was smart left turn and we faced two huge doors. The captain asked us to stand still, and the two leading privates stepped briskly forward and flung the two doors wide open. Facing us, at a distance of 20 metres, were two South Korean soldiers with rifles pointed in our direction, bayonets fixed; 20 metres behind them, up a control tower, was an American officer with a submachine gun. As our colonel took a well-rehearsed step to one side, the extrovert captain flung out his arm in a southern direction, sighted the US officer with his index finger and screamed:

'There you see foreign occupying troops on Korean soil.'

Neither Ron nor I felt like arguing at this point. The American – he seemed to be a lieutenant – took out a telescopic lens camera and calmly photographed Ron and myself. For some reason this irritated me momentarily, so I raised my camera and took a shot of him taking me. The North Korean captain howled with delight:

'Yes, take the pig's picture!' he screeched.

I took a couple more for good measure, wondering if I would ever again be allowed into the United States to visit my wife's parents. The American officer seemed unmoved. His photography done, he put down his camera on the parapet of the gun-tower and picked up his arm again. I winked at him, but nobody noticed. After that, we were taken down to the actual border line and were within 10 metres of the South Korean bayonets. The two sentries were as impassive as those Horse Guards in Whitehall. They could have been waiting for a train.

The descent of the fine marble steps was followed by a right wheel which led us to the long Nissen hut where the peace negotiations took place. Once inside, you really felt history lean on you. I was allowed to sit in the chair where Mark W. Clark signed the treaty and the captain obligingly took my picture. Ron struck a few poses, and we were given the North side of the peace talks for the previous two decades. The colonel had accompanied the captain and ourselves into the hut, where we stayed a good 20 minutes. The four privates eye-balled the South Korean sentries outside. Nobody looked like they were going to shoot, but I thought of the hatcheting and shivered a bit. It was getting dusk, but the captain finished his piece without switching on the lights of the hut.

We were escorted back to the bright lights of the big building, given various propaganda leaflets in English, and marched off to our cars. The captain shook my hand firmly and not unsympathetically as we said goodbye. I think he had hope – he allowed himself half a smile. Back in England, I received glossy books from North Korea until the end of the 1990s. I am no longer on their mailing list, but I have quite a collection of expensively produced volumes. I suppose that is what they spend their money on.

THE MEN'S FINAL

Amid the ubiquitous cultural idiosyncrasies and anomalies of our North Korean experience, the staging of the table tennis events progressed with some normality: one acceded to a world of sporting sanity each time one entered the stadium. In a way, the table tennis matches provided lucid intervals between the sessions of doctrinal conditioning that we experienced outside. And yet it was a scene in the stadium which, in the end, provided us with the deepest insight into North Korean behaviour and organization.

North Korea had a good table tennis team. They did quite well in these championships, though their best chances for medals lay in the individual events. They had two strong men in the Singles, while Li Song-suk, their star female player, was fully expected to win the Women's Singles. The stadium was packed each evening by Koreans, most of them drafted in from the countryside to give maximum support to their stars. They did not seem to understand the game, but they applauded vociferously as each Korean player won a point and hissed loudly when an opponent scored. This behaviour put us all off at first, but we got used to it and put it down to partisan enthusiasm. We had seen similar crowd comportment in Yugoslavia. The two Korean male stars were knocked out in the quarter-finals, but the brilliant, scowling Suk got through round after round in convincing fashion and eventually made the final of the Women's Singles.

The Finals, for men and women, were due to be played on the last Saturday. There was not a single seat vacant in the stadium – the crowd was more than 90 per cent Korean. The prospect of a Suk victory – and a gold medal – had raised rent-a-crowd's expectancy to fanatical heights. The rustic masses waited impatiently as the Women's Doubles, Men's Doubles and Mixed Doubles finals were played. There were no Korean participants. The last two finals scheduled were the Women's Singles and, of course, the Men's Singles.

There was a great hush as Suk took the table against a Chinese opponent. Suk was a sturdy figure, rather tall for a Korean, with long, black hair, fine wide cheekbones and a perennially frowning expression. The Chinese finalist, by contrast, was diminutive, dumpy and bespectacled. The stage was set for: the *Juche* heroine, a true model of the North Korean political ideal, who won her first game comfortably. The crowd nearly raised the roof off. The Chinese player, amid great hissing, unexpectedly won the second game. The crowd went deathly quiet as the Chinese led throughout the third and decisive game. Suk, though attacking brilliantly, was off her timing. Time and again she stamped her foot in rage as smashes missed the table. She lost.

The Chinese victor went up to the umpire for the usual handshake. Her coaches rushed to congratulate her. All Korean eyes were on Suk, who, hanging her head and ignoring her coach, walked slowly out of the arena. A new umpire arrived to take the Men's Final, which was to follow immediately. And then a strange thing happened. As Suk exited, the entire crowd rose quickly and evenly to its feet and vacated the stadium. One moment we were 5000 spectators, the next we were 300 foreigners. I had never witnessed anything like it at any sporting event that I had attended. Sports journalists of 40 years' experience said the same thing. Seiji Ono of Japan and Guo Yuehua of the People's Republic of China played the Men's Finals of the Pyongyang World Table Tennis Championships of 1979 to an empty stadium. It was exciting in the extreme, with Guo three times falling on the floor with violent stomach cramps and Ono eventually triumphing to end 12 years' Chinese domination in the event. Not one Korean was there to see it.

ADAMS' APPLES

In 1955 I worked as a news announcer for the Deutsche Welle – the German shortwave overseas service. We were housed in the Funkhaus Köln, a couple of hundred metres from Cologne's magnificent Gothic cathedral. Deutsche Welle broadcast news in English, French, Spanish, Italian and Portuguese, three times a day. The other English announcers besides myself were Barry Jones, an experienced radio journalist who had spent the war in Germany, and Fred Adams, a former British Army officer of great size. The French announcers were René Leurquin, a small, bounding Parisian, and Pierre d'Oncieu, a scholarly type from Tours. In general, we got on well together.

Adams used to eat an apple five minutes before each news bulletin. Someone had told him it had a calming effect on the nerves. It became a habit with him, and after a while he could not broadcast without one. He used to keep them in a big brown paper bag in the cupboard by the door. He never had fewer than six in reserve, and the whole office used to smell of apples.

One night, Jones got hungry on night shift and ate them all up. He didn't know how much Adams relied on them. On the morning shift, Adams didn't find out they were missing till five minutes before he had to go on air. He sent a secretary scuttling out to buy some, but she got stuck in the lift and didn't get back in time. He said he wouldn't go on the air, but they made him, and the bulletin was awful. Every time he made a mistake he coughed, and he coughed so much that his mother, who watched the news bulletin, wrote to ask if he was all right. Whenever you hear a news announcer cough, you must not think that this means he has a cold. It means that the technicians are flashing the sun into his eyes with a mirror or taking his shoes off or combing his hair in the middle. It is the only fun technicians get.

Dr Wesemann, the well-known head of Deutsche Welle, was not fond of announcers making mistakes. When Adams came up from the studio, he found a note on his typewriter.

'An apple a day keeps the *Doktor* away!'

It was not a kind note under the circumstances, and everybody kept out of Adams' way during the morning. He weighed 98 kilos. When Adams had gone home to sleep, I came on to do the 4.30 bulletin. Leurquin, the French announcer, was in the adjoining office. We wrote our bulletins as the stuff came in and went down at 4.25 to wait for the red light. It was then that we all noticed Leurquin was drunk. This had happened before and he was a good announcer when he was drunk, so we carried on with the news and he was all right – just. Every time he hiccupped, he did it at the end of a paragraph and cut himself off the air on each occasion with the press button.

We were due on again at 8pm, and I went up to the office to send some letters off. At 6pm they rang up from the canteen and told us that Leurquin had passed out over his fifth Steinhager. They carried him to his office but couldn't bring him round. D'Oncieu was on his holidays and Jones had gone to Hamburg for the day, so I would have to read the news in French, and we had to ring Adams up to help us out with the English. He had just eaten half a dozen apples and gone to bed.

I started doing the French news, and Adams took a taxi in and got going on the English. He had an apple in either pocket and was in a vicious mood. I had heard Leurquin and d'Oncieu drone away in French for a year, so I knew all the French words, but the French typewriter was unfamiliar and Leurquin snoring a few feet away distracted me. I had just got it finished when Leurquin came round and said he was going to read the news. He could hardly stand up and his eyes were crossed. The German editor tried to restrain him, so Leurquin went berserk and started wrecking the office. He was only a small chap, but it took four of them to lock him up in the lavatory. The din was terrible.

When news time came, I was feeling pretty nervous; Adams made a big sacrifice and gave me one of his apples. As we were going down in the lift, one of the editors shouted that Leurquin had broken loose, so we locked the studio door from the inside.

It was my turn first, and while I read we could hear Leurquin thumping on the studio door demanding entrance. Then he shattered the circular window in the door and tried to climb through, cutting his hands on the broken glass. After that he ran round the front and beat up the technician who was regulating the bulletin. Listeners in France must have asked themselves what all the strange noises were. I was glad when my five minutes were up.

While Adams read the English news, a full-scale battle was transpiring on the other side of the glass panel between Leurquin on the one hand and the technician, the assistant technician, a German news announcer and the German news editor on the other. We had ringside seats. It was the second awful broadcast Adams made in one day.

We were all Short Wave men, and Wesemann was proud of

us. There was a bitter feud going on at the time with the Medium Wave Service. It was all about studio rights and rehearsing facilities. There had been a lot of snooping. All the Medium Wave men were reporting the Short Wave men for this and that, and we were all reporting them. You had your work cut out to keep your record clean.

When Adams and I came out of the studio, the fight had just moved over to the corridor. There was a scarlet trail along the linoleum from Leurquin's cut hands; two pictures had been knocked down from the wall. Leurquin was sitting on top of the technician strangling him; the news editor and the assistant technician were trying to pull him off. The German announcer was sitting on the floor with his nose bleeding profusely; all five men were covered in blood. Leurquin was screaming at the top of his voice. The technician was desperately trying to free himself because he had to put on another tape to follow the news. The station signal had been repeating itself for a full three minutes. Adams wouldn't help because he said the news editor had taken his apples. While all this was going on, the Medium Wave Cultural Exchange Chief happened to pass by.

It just shows you can't be too careful.

BACK TO THE FUTURE

In the linear-active, industrialized Western cultures, time is seen as a road along which we proceed. Life is sometimes referred to as a 'journey'; death is often referred to as the 'end of the road'. We imagine ourselves as having travelled along the part of the road that is behind us (the past) and we see the untrodden path of the future stretching out in front of us.

Linear-oriented people do not regard the future as entirely unknowable, for they have already nudged it along certain channels by meticulous planning. American executives, with their quarterly forecasts, will tell you how much money they are going to make in the next three months. The Swiss station master will assure you, without any hesitation, that the train from Zurich to Luzern will leave at 09.03 tomorrow and arrive at exactly 10.05. He is probably right, too. Watches, calendars and computers are devices that not only encourage punctuality but also get us into the habit of working towards targets and deadlines. In a sense, we are 'making the future happen'. We cannot know everything (it would be disastrous for horse racing and detective stories), but we eliminate future unknowns to the best of our ability. Our personal programming tells us that over the next year we are going to get up at certain times, work so many hours, take vacations for designated periods, play tennis on Saturday mornings and pay our taxes on fixed dates.

Cyclic time is not seen as a straight road leading from our feet to the horizon, but as a curved one which in one year's time will lead us through 'scenery' and conditions very similar to what we experience at the present moment. Observers of cyclic time are less disciplined in their planning of the future, since they believe that it cannot be managed and that humans make life easier for themselves by 'harmonizing' with the laws and cyclic events of nature. Yet in such cultures a general form of planning is still possible, for many things are fairly regular and well understood.

Cultures observing both linear and cyclic concepts of time see the past as something we have put behind us and the future as something that lies before us. In Madagascar, the opposite is the case. The Malagasy imagine the future as flowing into the back of their heads, or passing them from behind, then becoming the past as it stretches out in front of them. The past is in front of their eyes because it is visible, known and influential. They can look at it, enjoy it, learn from it, even 'play' with it. The Malagasy people spend an inordinate amount of time consulting their ancestors, exhuming their bones, even partying with them.

By contrast, the Malagasy consider the future unknowable. It is behind their head where they do not have eyes. Their plans for this unknown area will be far from meticulous, for what can they be based on? Consequently, in Madagascar stocks are not replenished until shelves are empty, filling stations order gas only when they run dry, and hordes of would-be passengers at the airport find that, in spite of their tickets, in reality everybody is wait-listed. The actual assignation of seats takes place between the opening of the check-in desk and the (eventual) departure of the plane.

A few years ago, my wife and I spent a week in Madagascar's capital, Antananarivo. We had been introduced to Professor Andre Martin who held the Chair of History in the University and who kindly advised us with regard to local sightseeing. One of his suggestions was that we should visit Antsirana, a colourful market town about an hour's bus ride from the capital. A nice day's excursion, he said. We were very keen to follow his proposal and pleased to hear that a bus would leave for Antsirana at 9am the following morning. Give us plenty of time for touring, we thought. The next day we were gratified to find the appropriate bus already standing in the bus station, complete with driver, at 8.50. We paid the fare and hopped on board. There was no one else on the bus. The elderly driver seemed a friendly chap, glancing back to see we were comfortably seated.

At quarter past nine (we were still alone), I asked him when he thought the bus might leave.

'*Bientôt, monsieur*,' he replied with a smile.

At half past nine, after three more people had got on the bus, I asked him the same question.

'*Très bientôt, monsieur*,' he replied. The other passengers nodded in agreement and another 20 minutes passed as six more people filed into the vehicle. By the time they had got their tickets it was eight minutes to ten. Ten more people came scrambling on to the bus and obtained tickets.

I asked about departure a third time. The reply was definitely encouraging:

'*Dans deux minutes, monsieur*.'

Three final passengers hurtled aboard, taking the last seats. The bus left at ten, on the dot.

We arrived in Antsirana an hour late, but we had a good

time and returned to Antananarivo in the evening (no hurry).

During dinner, kindly offered by Professor Martin, we asked him if buses always left an hour late.

'You see, Monsieur Lewis, it is a matter of the situation triggering the event. The bus left at ten for two very good reasons. Firstly, it made economic sense, as the driver had a full complement. If he had left on time, only the two of you would have paid. The second reason why he left at ten is because that was the time most people had chosen to leave.'

ALBEROLA AND THE LANDLORDS

In 1966 I was appointed to the post of Executive Director Berlitz Schools of East Asia and instructed to open the area's first school in Tokyo.

When I left for Japan, I was accompanied by Rafael Alberola, assistant to the CEO of Berlitz in New York, who judged that Alberola would be of invaluable help to me in negotiating school premises in the Japanese capital. There was a reason for this: Alberola, though of French nationality and blond and blue-eyed, had been born and spent his first 25 years in Casablanca, Morocco. Though decidedly Nordic in appearance and, in Japanese eyes, a smartly dressed American executive, he had little in common with either of these cultures. Though vaguely French, he was an Arab at heart. When you have been brought up amid the souks and bazaars of a Moroccan metropolis, you develop a certain cynicism vis-à-vis a fellow human being with whom you have to negotiate. Bargaining and haggling are part and parcel of Moroccan street life. Even in a strange culture, Alberola had no doubt he could stand on his own feet.

After arriving in Tokyo, Alberola and I took half a day off, recovering from jetlag, and then busied ourselves looking for space. There was plenty available in the central part of the city. We looked at floors in the Ginza, Akasaka, Yūrakuchō and Ōtemachi. Rents were high, though they later became much higher. The most interesting experience for me at this time was to observe how Alberola negotiated with the Japanese landlords. He knew nothing about Japanese negotiating principles, so he applied Arab ones. The conversations usually went like this:

Alberola:	This building is totally empty.
Japanese:	You see, it is a new building.
Alberola:	There seem to be so many in Tokyo. Who'll rent them all?
Japanese:	This is a very good location.
Alberola:	We need a big sign on the front of the building.
Japanese:	We are quite happy to let you put one up, but you may have problems with the authorities.
Alberola:	It's a major condition for renting. What's the rent for the first floor?
Japanese:	700,000 yen.
Alberola:	Far too high – we have much better offers.
Japanese:	This is an excellent location.
Alberola:	What's the real rent?
Japanese:	I beg your pardon?
Alberola:	What's the rent for me? Just be realistic – I can walk away from this.
Japanese:	I can discuss the matter with my colleagues. Perhaps we could reduce the rent by 5 per cent on certain conditions.
Alberola:	Let's use 500,000 yen as a base figure for the time being. But in fact, I only need half the floor.
Japanese:	Which half?
Alberola:	I guess more people will see us if we take the front half on the main street.

Japanese:	Naturally.
Alberola:	I take it the front half would cost exactly half of the total.
Japanese:	This we must discuss.
Alberola:	If we base our figure on 500,000, the front half should cost 250,000.
Japanese:	However, the front half is better space. There must be a premium for this.
Alberola:	Then how would you split the rent?
Japanese:	Something like 60 per cent for the half on the street and 40 per cent for the back half.
Alberola:	I'll take the back half (the quiet half he wanted all the time).

This particular landlord was so miffed that he didn't rent to us at all. He did, however, prolong the dialogue for a week or so.

It was quite a different situation when we tried to negotiate the Monte Carlo building in the Ginza. The president of the company that owned the building had checked on the Berlitz name back in the United States and kindly agreed to give us an interview. He was in his late seventies, spoke no English, and had provided a timid interpreter. The old gentleman spelled out, in the correct, prescribed manner, the attributes and benefits of the building. It was almost new, had an impeccable address, enjoyed a good reputation, was conveniently located for all kinds of transport, was, in short, a *prestige* building and had many facilities such as restaurants, a travel bureau, a bank and others which he proceeded to list. His well-balanced account took 10–15 minutes.

When he had finished, Alberola asked him what the rent was. One million yen a month, replied the president through his young interpreter. Offer him half a million, snapped Alberola to the hapless translator. The young man swallowed hard and took some time to muster up the courage necessary to interpret Alberola's proposal. When this had been done, the president rose from his chair, placed his hands on both knees, bowed slightly as he said, *'Domo, arigato gozaimasu'* (thank you very much) and left the room followed by his nervous subordinate. 'He'll come back with 750, you'll see,' confided Alberola to me.

The president did not come back, neither did the interpreter. We sat there alone for half an hour until a young girl popped her head round the door and asked if we had a problem. No problem said Alberola. Ten minutes later she came again and beckoned to us from the doorway to ask us to follow her. She took us to the lift, kindly pressing the button designating the ground floor, and took the ride with us. As we departed, she bowed much lower than the president had done.

29

MR KISHI'S TABLE

In 1966 England won the World Cup, and I was looking for furniture in Tokyo where I was to live for the next five years.

Tokyo has wonderful department stores with a lot on view and I frequented the home furnishing floors of Mitsukoshi, Takashimaya, Seibu, Hankyu and Matsuzaka. It was while I was looking for a table that I gained my first insight into the nature of Japanese courtesy. I had spotted a lovely Danish teak dining table, just the right size for our house, in the Takashimaya department store. I asked the shop assistant how much it cost – it was 66,000 yen. I was eager to snap it up, but the assistant explained that he could not sell it to me, as a certain Mr Kishi had 'reserved' it. I accepted this explanation, but was surprised, when still hunting around Takashimaya two weeks later, to see the table still there. I approached the same assistant and enquired about the fate of the table. Mr Kishi had still not made up his mind, was the answer. 'Had Mr Kishi put down a deposit on the table?' was my next question. 'No, he had not.' Then how do you know he is serious about buying it? Mr Kishi is a valued customer. Could I put down a deposit on the table, in case Mr Kishi decides not to buy it? That would not be necessary, my interest had been registered.

The following week, I tried again. Could the assistant please ask the invisible Mr Kishi to fix a date for a decision, as I was holding off buying another table until the fate of this one was decided. He was afraid that was not possible; Mr Kishi should not be pushed into making hasty decisions.

'How long had the table been standing there?' I asked.

'Three months,' was the reply.

The days passed, the weather got hotter, my determination to secure the table increased. I tried out a variety of strategies with the gentle, but firm, store assistant. Could he give me Mr Kishi's telephone number so that I could ascertain his intentions personally? Unfortunately, that would not be possible; besides, he was not sure the store had the number. Then how did he communicate with Mr Kishi about the table? From time to time Mr Kishi would come into the store and look at it, I was told. Could I waylay him in the store one day? That would be difficult, as one never knew when he would come and inspect. I have 66,000 yen here in cash in an envelope, will you take it now and make sure of the sale? The assistant smiled a smile of embarrassment – he could not take the money.

Knowing the Japanese as I now do, I reckon I broke every possible social convention surrounding the delicate rules of Japanese customer relations, exercise of patience, practice of courtesy and avoidance of direct propositions. In later months I shuddered at what must have seemed, in Japanese eyes, my uneducated bluntness, even brashness. My humiliation was complete one morning when, as I gazed at the coveted teak top, the assistant sidled up to me and informed me of Mr Kishi's decision. Though he greatly prized the table, he had decided, in view of the foreign guest's persistence and eagerness to purchase it, to renounce his right to buy. He was very pleased to let me have it in the hope that it would bring many years of enjoyment and aesthetic pleasure. I felt like a heel, paid like a shot and scuttled off with my prize. Twenty-five years later, the admirable table is still in use and looks like it did the day I bought it. So much for Danish workmanship. I never met the honourable Mr Kishi, but still think of him with fondness and admiration. He and the shop assistant were true Japanese gentlemen.

IN JAPAN

Japan is perhaps the most popular Asian country with Westerners, particularly among Americans and other English speakers. In spite of this, it is the country which provides Westerners with the greatest number of cultural surprises. Japan was isolated from the rest of the world from 1600 to 1853 and during this period developed an inward-looking, tightly knit society that maintained certain standards of behaviour uncommon in the West. One of their outstanding traits is the unbelievably high level of courtesy. It is well known that the Japanese never say 'no'. My daughter, as a 10-year-old girl, spent six weeks in Japan as the guest of a friend of ours, Yoshio Miyake. Miyake-san took Caroline, along with his own daughter, down to Shimonoseki, where they went to dinner at a splendid seafood restaurant right by the sea.

When they were seated inside, the restaurant manager, who knew the Miyakes well, came to pay his respects and to welcome Caroline. As a special honour she was shown the kitchen (all this in Japanese) and led to a large tank in which swam a dozen or more beautiful fish. Caroline was asked which fish she liked best and she pointed one out – a lovely pink one. They returned to their table. A couple of minutes later Caroline saw the cook walking round with the nice pink fish in a net. She asked Miyake-san why he was doing this, and Miyake explained that the cook would hit the fish on the head and that soon they would be eating it.

On hearing this, my tender-hearted daughter burst into tears and asked them to save the fish. On such occasions, Japanese move quickly. Miyake-san streaked across the room, the cook's hammer was arrested in mid-air, the manager hurried out to reassure the English guest. When Caroline asked for the fish to be returned to the sea, there was no hesitation. In the rays of the Shimonoseki setting sun, a solemn procession walked across the sandy beach to the sea – the cook, carrying the pink fish in his net, Caroline behind him, then Miyake-san and his daughter, then the restaurant manager bringing up the rear. Pity we did not get a photograph.

Mandatory Japanese politeness explores realms of courtesy that seem funny to Westerners. My wife and I were having dinner at the house of some Japanese friends in Atami. The dinner party consisted of about 16 people – Japanese, British and American. In the middle of the main course the phone rang, and our hostess went to answer it. She spoke Japanese, which most of us understood, and we listened idly to what she said. Someone was obviously asking her about property prices in Atami, for she indicated what she had paid for her villa, how prices increased as you went up the slope and how they decreased if you went too far up or too far to the left-hand side. She discussed inflation and the advantages of investing in property, as well as the general state of the property market in Japan and in Atami in particular. She was a knowledgeable woman and the call took 10 minutes. Finally, with a lot of bowing on the phone, she concluded the conversation and hurried back to the table with her apologies to the guests. 'Who was that?' asked one of her friends. 'Wrong number,' she replied.

SUMO WRESTLER

Legendary Japanese courtesy also extends to sporting arenas. When the Arsenal Football Club visited Japan in 1967, Chris McDonald, a well-known Englishman resident in Tokyo, gave a lavish quasi all-night party for the Arsenal team, officials and a large number of invited guests.

The party turned out to be a memorable event. Chris had invited not only a dozen or so very attractive Japanese women, but also four or five top sumo wrestlers in their splendid dark blue kimonos. Several of these men weighed over 150 kilos – about twice the bulk of the average Arsenal footballer. They were invariably dignified and withdrawn, with their splendid blue-back topknots, hooded eyes and ham-like hands. They could not, of course, speak any English, but as the evening progressed they established a friendly dig-in-the-ribs rapport with some of the more outgoing Arsenal players – Neale, Graham and McLintock in particular – and downed a considerable number of beers with them.

Under a certain amount of intoxicating influence, one or two of the Arsenal players began to fancy their chances of throwing one of these sumo wrestlers in man-to-man combat. The sumo champions laughingly refused contact, but in the end one of them – Varna we called him – agreed to have a few friendly tussles with some of the footballers. A space was cleared in one of Chris's large tatami-mat rooms, and some good-natured jousting began. One or two of the bigger Arsenal players – Furnell and Radford, I believe they were – were gently deposited on the tatami after two or three minutes' mock struggle by Varna. Finally, Frank Mclintock, the not so heavy but certainly athletic club captain, strode forward to take up the challenge. After what seemed to be a fierce encounter, Varna was suddenly thrown backwards down on the mat, defeated by a jubilant Frank. The Arsenal players cheered their skipper to the rafters, even Bertie Mee, the Arsenal manager, looked impressed. Chris and I tried to keep straight faces; it was harder for us than for the impassive blue-clad row of wrestlers looking on. Varna was a warm-hearted gentleman of Japan.

We were eating Japanese style, sitting on tatami – the house had big square rooms; about twenty of us surrounded one particular table covered in dishes of all kinds, including mountains of fruit. By midnight, the main dishes had been consumed – one had to marvel at the capacity of some of the wrestlers. Rice dishes would be piled one foot high for them and would quickly disappear. Finally, only bananas were left and most of us had one. Everyone sat around quietly for a while, drinking beer and sake. Then Takanohana, the most celebrated Sumo champion present, picked up the big bowl containing 21 bananas and went round the table to each guest in turn offering the fruit. He knew the operative word in English. To each person he said 'Banana?' In each case the answer was a polite 'No thank you'. Takanohana deposited the bowl on the table again, contemplated the scene for another 30 seconds, then ate the 21 bananas in one-minute flat.

RICE PUDDING IN FUKUOKA

A few days later Arsenal was due to play an All-Japan XI in the city of Fukuoka on the island of Kyushu. The team was housed in a local hotel. Hotel staff in Fukuoka are much less used to foreigners than their counterparts in Tokyo or Kobe, and there was some nervousness about the preparation of food for the footballers. Arsenal, in fact, had a set pre-match meal which apparently never varied. It consisted of two courses: a thin beefsteak and chips, followed by rice pudding. This meal had to be consumed exactly three hours before kick-off.

The match was scheduled to begin at 2pm, so everyone assembled in the dining room just before 11 in the morning. A large hotel kitchen was adjacent to the dining room, and we could see through the open hatches a dozen or so cooks scampering around. The beefsteak and chips appeared in fine style and were devoured by the players among murmurs of appreciation. The empty plates were removed by the hotel staff and replaced by a large bowl of rice for each player. Japanese eat their boiled rice, white and sticky, with no additives of any kind. That is how they like it – hot, pure and tasteless. There was some perplexity, then howls of protest from the Arsenal team: 'This is not rice pudding!'

One of the assistant managers came running along to see what could possibly be wrong with the beautiful rice, and Chris McDonald tried to explain to him, in fluent Japanese, the concept of English rice pudding. Now 'pudding' is not a word that translates readily into Japanese. When they use the English word themselves (sometimes they write it 'puddy'), they could mean trifle or cake or almost anything sweet. Rice pudding in Japan is simply an alien concept. They would no more pour milk, cream and sugar on rice than we would put jam on chips. Chris did very well explaining what was required and the assistant manager trotted off to the kitchen to issue further directives.

When he came back, it was with bad news. The chefs had refused outright to cook the rice with milk and sugar. Chris reasoned with him, but distressed though he was, he was power-less to sway the cooks: they were adamant. The fact is that Japanese people attach much more symbolism to rice than English people do to fish and chips. Both are national institu-tions, but good Japanese – and professional cooks at that – do not tamper with a 2000-year-old culinary tradition, with all its religious implications, for the sake of a miserable football match against uncouth barbarians.

Bertie Mee and Don Howe, the Arsenal manager and trainer, were now glancing nervously at their watches, for the holy three-hour digestion period had now been eroded by a good 20 minutes. Mee muttered something about cancelling the match, which sent the four Japanese Football Association (JFA) officials present into transports of untrammelled panic as the stadium was already half full and people were still pouring through the gates. The JFA men dragged in the hotel manager and reported to him the seriousness of the situation. He rushed off to the kitchen with a worried look on his face; he looked even more careworn when he came back: he was not able to budge the chefs.

By now we had all the ingredients of an impasse. No rice pudding, no match, said Bertie. Loss of face on the English side now equalled that of the faithful-to tradition Japanese cooks. It was a lose–lose situation, especially for the JFA. 'How about some nice bananas?' suggested the JFA vice-president. Don Howe laughed derisively. All the Japanese tittered, too – only in Japan tittering means extreme embarrassment. It was nearly half past eleven.

Chris found the way out. Rushing to the kitchen, he grabbed

bowls of sugar and jugs of milk. The rice was still there, luke-warm in the bowls on the table. Everybody, me included, began to spoon sugar and pour milk into the rice bowls. The players stirred it all up with the chopsticks, the JFA men fetched spoons and soon there was pleasant chomping all round. In the middle of all this I happened to glance towards the kitchen. There, through the open hatches, were lined up all the chefs and their staff, arms defiantly folded, watching open-mouthed the sacri-legious, unhallowed ritual. Arsenal won 1–0.

RED CARDS

Japanese football crowds are polite in the extreme. There are no soccer hooligans in Japan, either on the pitch or on the terraces. Gentlemanly conduct and a sense of fair play are in evidence on the field. Cheering or shouting is very restricted. Good play, on either side, is generally appreciated by hand clapping.

When I lived in Japan, I played football for several years and was able to observe their behaviour from this additional perspective. If a Japanese player kicks or fouls you, he apologizes on the spot, always poker-faced. He will foul you again – and apologize again. They are not rough players – on the contrary, they are generally fair and admire correctness of comportment. Their referees are indeed humorous. In one match, one of our players – a Frenchman – fouled consistently and the Japanese referee showed him the yellow card; after the next bad foul he showed him the red card and the man had to leave the field. The Frenchman's brother, who was on the touchline, was an excitable individual and he went on the field to remonstrate with the referee. As he gesticulated in Gallic fashion, the

Japanese showed him the yellow card. When he continued to perorate, the referee showed him the red card and led him gently off the field by the elbow.

Japanese courtesy is so persistent that I had to ask myself: if a Japanese really wants to insult someone, what does he say? It was explained to me that when this is the case, he shows his displeasure by actions, not words. For instance he will arrive five minutes late for a meeting; he will place you behind the driver in his car; he will treat your business card roughly (pretending not to read it, throwing it casually on the table, slipping it into his pocket or, even worse, drawing on it!). Another Japanese will be infuriated by such actions, though his code of behaviour does not allow him to complain. For the Westerner, who would not even know that he was being insulted, such Japanese tricks, when eventually understood, appear indescribably funny, though the intent is exactly the opposite. We even begin to like the Japanese when they behave in this way. How much more pleasant it is to be contraried in such a harmless manner than to be cursed or sworn at!

A Japanese woman, when upset, has to be even more subtle in expressing her annoyance. It is not often a wife will engage in a war of words with her husband. On returning from work, however, he may find that she has made a flower arrangement that is not to his taste or one that is artistically flawed.

In the course of time I witnessed an admirable example of an effective Japanese insult to a visiting Korean football team. On this occasion the Republic of (South) Korea were playing Japan and their players had been in the country for a few days' training prior to the match. Japanese and Koreans do not get on together particularly well (Japanese go so far as to call their neighbours 'garlic eaters'), and the Korean officials had found endless grounds for complaint about the training facilities, the hotel accommodation, food and so on. The JFA had shown great patience during the week, trying to meet some rather unreasonable demands and maintaining politeness at all times. The Koreans gave them little thanks for the troubles. I was friendly with Shunichiro Okano, the manager of the Japanese national side, and I was aware that all the Japanese officials were seething at the Koreans' behaviour. This was a match they had to win at all costs.

The intense rivalry between the two countries produced a full stadium half an hour before kick-off. As the sun set, the stadium lights went on and an air of expectation could be felt on the terraces. The Japanese crowd, rather unusually, was on edge. The two teams took the field for the opening ceremony. Keeping character, the crowd refrained from booing the visitors (as would have happened in Europe). First the band began to play the Korean anthem and the Korean flag slowly ascended its flagpole. There was sudden tumult. Half a dozen Korean officials rushed onto the pitch, shrieked wildly at their players, who ran off the field as fast as they could, back to their changing room. The Japanese team remained standing in their line-up. The crowd maintained silence and then, perceptibly, murmured in a subdued, contented manner. What had happened? The JFA, unpardonably, had confused the flags and national anthems of the two Koreas. Kim Il-sung's North Korea banner fluttered at the top of the flagpole of the biggest soccer stadium in Tokyo. JFA officials suitably panicked. Kim's flag was hastily lowered, the ROK flag went up and the band hastily played another tune. After 20 minutes or so the Koreans were persuaded to take the field again.

TIE-BREAKER – JAPANESE STYLE

On English language summer courses one had to organize an evening social programme to keep the students occupied. One of the most popular events was the weekly International Song Contest, which never lacked participants in quantity, though one could not always say that of the quality. Entrants were allowed to sing (solo or with others), dance or play an instrument. Usually they sang in groups. In fact, the standard varied enormously, and we never quite knew what we were getting next. In general – and perhaps surprisingly – the Spaniards and Italians usually came last. Their 'choirs' were often too big, uncoordinated and frequently raucous. They enjoyed themselves perhaps more than anyone else, but rarely won any prizes. The Arabic style of singing, though soulful, was something of an acquired taste – they never won either. Ireland, Scotland and Sweden often triumphed. England, France and Germany were kind of middling. My friend Ladislav sang 'O sole mio' in Czech week after week and usually got third prize. But the best, on the whole, were the Japanese.

Japanese people at parties, whether at home or abroad, show no hesitation in contributing musical numbers when they are asked to. With them it is a kind of collective social obligation. They are not all particularly talented, but they always put on a good show. Also, they hate to lose. One night we had double-headers – that is to say that each country contributed two numbers. It was known that the Spaniards had an excellent flamenco singer who was bound to score good points in the second round. Spain also started with a fine guitarist in the first round. The Japanese, who were the only ones with a chance of beating the Spaniards, countered with an elegant fan dancer in round one and an exquisite trio singing impeccable close melody in the second round. The flamenco singer did her stuff, and after two rounds Japan and Spain were exactly equal with eighteen and a half points each.

When this happened, we used a tie-breaker, where each tying country was allowed to put on one more number to decide the issue, with a different performer. Everyone knew that the Spaniards had a fine baritone singer left, and he thrilled the audience – and the judges – with some Aragonese ballad which nearly lifted the roof off. Surely that was it!

A slender, willowy young Japanese woman, unnoticed before, shyly took the stage. She sang a song in Japanese. We had never heard anything like it on our courses. Her voice was mellow magic, her features angelic. It was clearly a love song. The judges could not understand the words, but that was of little import. They knew class when they heard it. She got 10 out of 10, and Japan won. What intrigued me about the whole thing was the subtlety of the Japanese contingent's plot. The young woman was a well-known professional nightclub singer back in Tokyo. The Japanese, banking on the first two rounds ending in a tie, had held her back for the coup de grâce.

FIRST NIGHT IN JAPAN

My elderly parents (mid-seventies) finally made the momentous decision to come to Japan, where my wife and I and two children had been living for six months. They arrived just before Christmas.

A strange incident occurred on the night of their arrival in Tokyo. After a late family dinner, we all went to bed – Jane and I, the children, my parents in the three main bedrooms, and

Haruko, the maid, to her own room. At eight the next morning we assembled for breakfast and Haruko did us proud serving bacon and eggs in the prescribed English manner. As we were finishing breakfast, she suddenly burst into tears. We were astounded, as she was normally a most equable young woman, but at that point I noticed a cut on the side of her nose. At the very same instant I caught a glimpse of my briefcase lying on the grass in the middle of the garden! Haruko sobbed away for five minutes or so and then, in Japanese, told her story.

About 4am a burglar, wearing a mask, had entered her room. As she awoke, he held a knife to her throat and threatened to kill her if she made a sound. When he was satisfied that she was too terrified to betray him, he went through the items in the living room. There was little to steal apart from a small amount of money in my briefcase, which he took out with him as he went. As a further precaution he returned to poor Haruko's room deliberately gave her a small nick on the nose with his knife and told her he would surely disfigure her if she raised the alarm in the following couple of hours. Shaken, Haruko cowered in her room for three hours or so, then got up and prepared our breakfast as it had been ordered. Finally, she broke down.

The event revealed so much about the Japanese character, especially the young woman's fortitude. The police were called – 17 of them arrived, and 17 pairs of shoes were lined up outside our front door. The house was fingerprinted from top to bottom. Haruko was cross-examined and re-cross-examined. The rest of us marvelled at the manpower involved. They came again, three or four days in a row. Haruko had a plaster on her nose for a couple of weeks. We felt for her and loved her. The story had a happy ending: not only did they catch the burglar (six months later) but the bright-eyed 25-year-old sergeant in charge of the investigation later proposed to Haruko and they were married in 1968, when she had given the matter due consideration. They have three children.

That was my parents' first night in Japan. I had to assure them that it didn't happen every night.

31

FIRE IN SHOTO-CHO

The only house we ever lived in in Japan was a three-bedroomed bungalow in the residential district of Shoto-cho on the hill above Shibuya station. Though we did not know it when we rented it, it was one of Tokyo's most exclusive suburbs, convenient for transport, quiet day or night, and home to half a dozen foreign embassies. The house itself was made of wood, Japanese-style with a small back garden containing a dozen bamboo trees.

Our street was about 100 metres long with about 10 modest bungalows of different periods on each side. The numbers – Tokyo fashion – were in accordance with the date the house had been built. We were number 16 but our closest neighbours were 4 and 21. It was fun trying to find someone's house when you came the first time.

One house in the street, about 15 metres further down from us, on the left-hand side, was different from the others. It was two-storey, built on a kind of bank 3 metres higher than the road and had a nice front garden, as well as back. The front garden had several exquisite Japanese-style bushes and two or three small trees.

The house was the biggest in the street, but also made of wood. It was owned by a rich gentleman of middle age whom we saw leave for work every morning in a black Toyota with a smart driver and white lace covers of the back of the seats. The gentleman was reputed to be an important company director. He nodded politely to any neighbours he drove past, Japanese or foreigners alike. We never had the pleasure of meeting him but sensed that he was an agreeable personality.

One night, when we had lived there for over a year, his house burned down. At two in the morning we were awakened by, first, the smell of burning wood, then a series of shouts and shortly afterwards the shrill 'Nee-naw' of the fire engine. Not surprisingly we jumped out of bed, threw on a robe and opened the front door. The fire brigade had a hopeless job in terms of saving the house. A wall of flames illuminated the whole length of the street, the walls of the house were already largely consumed, black smoke billowed from the flaming ruin, and the fierce crackle of the conflagration made conversation difficult. About 50 people, including the owner of the burning house and his family, populated the street. The firemen kept everybody away from the building – it was obvious nothing could be salvaged. Fortunately, no one had perished. Around four in the morning we went back to bed and caught a few hours' sleep.

The following day we were undecided as to what to do. In England we would have sought out our unfortunate neighbours, commiserated with them, offered any kind of help they might consider appropriate, including substituting any household items then needed urgently, or even providing shelter if necessary. Although we were relatively new to Japan, we knew there would be a certain protocol to follow as the regimented Japanese society has a fairly fixed formula for any event or crisis. We obviously could not offer any financial help; we did not know the man, and he was clearly a lot richer than we were. It was unlikely than anything we possessed in the house could be of service to him – his dwelling had been burned to the ground and he was currently elsewhere. We resolved to keep our eyes open for his return, hasten to express our sympathy when he or his family would appear, and ask if there was anything we could do. We were very much aware that we should not pity the family in any way as we were only too sensitive to the Japanese preoccupation with loss of face.

It was while we were discussing these prospects that we heard a gentle knock on our front door. It was 9.30 in the morning. On opening the door, we were confronted by our rich neighbour, accompanied by his driver in full uniform. The latter was bearing gifts, literally. Our neighbour bowed low to my wife and myself and said in impeccable English: 'I would like to apologize most sincerely for the trouble we caused you last night. The noise and smell were terrible; you probably could not sleep at all. In order to compensate you for your discomfort I would be most happy if you would kindly accept these small gifts.' At this point, the driver pressed a beautifully wrapped box into my hands and gave a similar one to my wife. The neighbour and his driver then bowed low, thanked us with fixed smiles and passed on to the next house to repeat the ritual. I knew what it was to be at a loss for words. What could we shout after them? – 'Don't mention it', 'We are so sorry your house burned down', 'You shouldn't have given us anything'?

It turned out that our neighbour's action was in conformity with that of a prosperous person whose misfortune had caused such a commotion in the immediate neighbourhood. Though our reaction was nonplussed and inadequate at the time, my wife and I were able to send our neighbour a note of thanks a few days later, as did the 18 other similarly compensated families who lived on the street. Just another lesson in Japanese behaviour.

TAKADA COMES HOME

In 1984 the World Skiing Championships were held in Lahti, Finland, where I officiated as an interpreter. I was involved in several events, but the one in which I developed keenest interest was the ski jumping competition. This event, usually dominated by Norwegian, Finnish and Austrian contestants, was of special interest in 1984, as Japan, not normally among the top rankings, had entered a young and daring team. Pushing themselves to the limit, they had attracted the Nordic crowd's attention by good jumping, risky attitudes and one or two falls.

As I was planning to go to Japan in the years that followed, I kind of attached myself to the Japanese team while they were in Lahti, helping out with one or two minor matters such as diet and travel arrangements. The manager of the team was a handsome 60-year-old Japanese, Seiji Takada, reputed to be the president of a large and prosperous pearl company from the north of Japan. It appeared that his company had financed the participation of the ski-jumping team in the world championships and had plans to make Japan a future force in the jumping event. Takada himself threw himself wholeheartedly into all the proceedings surrounding the championships. He was obviously a person who enjoyed life to the full – training with the team, and gaily interviewing with the numerous press representatives who were enamoured by his enthusiasm, charisma and colourful English. He met the mayor of Lahti and attended all the functions the city laid on. He laughed and smiled at everyone, even when two of his athletes took a tumble. He was a real character.

Years later, when I contacted him in Japan, he came to Tokyo to see me, gave me a pearl tie-pin and a jade ashtray, and exhibited the same lust for life and engaging humour that he had demonstrated before the Finnish public.

When I was about to leave Japan a year or two later, I had lunch with an old Japan hand, a veteran correspondent at the Press Club. He was surprised I knew Takada and told me a story about him. He was indeed rich and influential and had inherited the Presidency of the Takada Pearl Co. from his father. There had been five sons, and all were called up in the Armed Forces after Pearl Harbor. Seiji was the youngest, aged 20. One son was killed in Burma, another fell in Bataan. The third son died in a kamikaze plane, the fourth perished in Okinawa. Seiji, who was awarded a medal for bravery, was taken prisoner in the Philippines and was repatriated in 1946. On returning home, he was greeted at the front door by his father, who snapped, 'Well, why have you come home?'

A PLACE FOR KATO

When I returned to the UK from Japan in 1971, I was given an introduction to Tadao Kato, the Japanese ambassador to the Court of St James, by Chris McDonald with whom I had played football in the Yokohama County and Athletic Club. Kato himself was a former footballer of considerable repute and welcomed me warmly. We had lunch together a couple of times, and my wife and I were invited to Japanese Embassy functions for the rest of his tenure.

He was a very relaxed and likeable individual, still athletic in build with fine manly features. I was indeed sorry to hear that about five years after returning to Japan he died in his sixties. It was not until a decade later that I heard of another incident in his career which touched on my interest in the cross-cultural field.

Tad Kato, as he was known by his English friends, had been quite a brilliant student at Cambridge University, which he entered just before the war. He was of course in his college soccer team and belonged to one or two student clubs, as was the norm. He was immensely popular with students and staff, not least with his elderly tutor, Jack Ainsdale. The latter was convinced that Kato would go far and gave him special attention with regard to his studies. Tad progressed well, got good marks and relished his Cambridge years.

On 7 December 1941, the Imperial Japanese Air Force bombed Pearl Harbor and sank half the American fleet on anchor. The next day Japan, the United States and Great Britain were at war. Jack Ainsdale rushed round the campus and grabbed Tad Kato, who had not heard the news. How does one break that kind of news? Ainsdale, a sensitive academic with a heart of gold, took it upon himself to inform his student in the most delicate way possible – a masterpiece of English coded speech.

Taking the young Japanese by the arm, he drew him gently into the college chapel and led him up to an alcove near the altar, where a tablet had been erected to honour those college students who had fallen in the two world wars. There were two dozen names on the tablet. Ainsdale and his student contemplated the list for a while, before the professor put his arm round the Japanese's shoulder and said softly: 'There will be a place for you, Kato.'

THE RENT IN VOLGOGRAD

In 1991 I was approached by two Russians from Volgograd (formerly Stalingrad) who wished to set up a language school in that city in conjunction with Richard Lewis Communications (RLC), a company specializing in language teaching and inter-cultural consulting. One was Alexander Kosov, an assistant professor at the University of Volgograd; the other was Antonina Zhilin, a member of the Russian Parliament and a lady of considerable means, who seemed quite capable and willing to provide any necessary capital.

It was not in RLC's interest to get involved with the rouble economy – we all knew what a state of confusion Russia was in at that time – but I was certainly interested in a school which could teach Russian in Russia, the fees for which would be collected in hard currency in the West. Basically, we were not interested in teaching English to Russians in Russia.

As both Alexander and Antonina proved reliable, I was willing to pursue the project; Kosov subsequently came to Riversdown, the exclusive language school in Hampshire where I was a director, took some training in the RLC method and, with my help, wrote an RLC manual in modern post-Soviet Russian. I had indicated to our Russian colleagues that, if we were to send Western businessmen to Russia on immersion courses, the actual teaching would be the least of our problems;

the success of the venture would depend largely on the quality of food and accommodation we provided. There are many intensive courses in Russian offered in the universities of Moscow and St Petersburg; university hostel accommodation is, however, completely unsuitable for executives.

I told Alexander and Antonina that they must find four- or five-star rooms in Volgograd and guarantee excellent food; I did not consider it likely that they would succeed. They did, however, and in an unusual manner. When Eisenhower became President of the United States, he expressed a wish to visit the battlefield of Stalingrad which, as we all know, witnessed one of the major turning points of the Second World War. The municipal authorities in Stalingrad (now called Volgograd) prepared for his visit by building a private villa in a compound, with eight suites (for Eisenhower's retinue), a reception room and cooking quarters. Each suite, luxuriously appointed, contained a bedroom, a study, a large kitchen and a bathroom with toilet.

In the end Eisenhower changed his mind and did not go. Nobody quite knew what to do with the building, so it was used in an ad hoc manner by a variety of dignitaries when they passed through the lower Volga region. These had included Khrushchev, Brezhnev, Charles de Gaulle, Fidel Castro, President Najibullah of Afghanistan, President Nazarbayev of Kazakhstan Princess Anne and Elizabeth Rehn, the Finnish minister of defence! Most of the time it remained empty.

When Alexander Kosov proposed this as the school location, I thought I was being exposed to a Russian sense of humour. He was, however, quite serious and when I found out that it could be rented for $500 a month, so was I. The following January, I flew down to Volgograd and inspected the building, which was in good shape. After some discussion with our friends, I decided the best way to solve the food question was to send them part of the fee paid in hard currency and entrust three or four Russian housewives to buy what was needed in the markets and cook it at home. Students would be taught, sleep and have breakfast in the villa and eat the remaining meals with Volgograd families; in practice, the system worked fine. We subsequently sent various executives from the UK, Sweden, Finland and Germany to Volgograd. Kosov did a good job and we were able to satisfy our clientele.

The volume of our Russian business is fairly small, but I write of this venture on account of some of the interesting insights that I was given into the state of affairs in Russia in the period of the Soviet break-up. There was, for instance, the question of ownership. Who owned our building, who fixed the rent and to whom was it paid? Even Alexander Kosov, who had to pay it, was a little woolly about it. Up to the Gorbachev era, the villa had been Soviet property. When the Soviet Union was dissolved, Soviet assets reverted to the various states so that in theory it was administered by the Russian state. As committees were changing fast, the link between Moscow and far-off properties tended to get lost, especially in cases where regular rents were not being collected. The Communist Party got into the act wherever they could, but as it was in the process of being smashed by Yeltsin, administering empty buildings in Volgograd was low on their list of priorities. The city council was in the picture somehow, but did not possess any title to the villa, which continued to be well maintained by a caretaker and a cook, possibly his wife, who laid on meals for the pair of them in the presidential kitchen as well as cooking breakfasts for our students. Volgograd was heaving with Russian, Georgian and Armenian entrepreneurs, but they had bigger fish to fry. Nobody could buy the property as nobody knew who owned it. A communist who had been around when the last dignitaries visited had since disappeared. It was unclear who was paying the caretaker and the cook, who also did the gardening.

In these ephemeral and unballasted circumstances the calculation of rent seemed to be up to Kosov and me more than anybody else. I know that we arrived at the figure of $500 a month with considerable ease. We had only the caretaker to discuss it with, and he kept nodding so hard I thought his head would drop off. Rent in advance? Of course not. What if it took us a while to rustle up students? The landlords would be understanding. Who were the current landlords? The answer was so nebulous and protracted that even Dostoyevsky would have had trouble with it. Who would collect the rent? He, the caretaker, would. He would pass it on through the proper channels. Yes, Mr Kosov would get a receipt. Yes, hard currency would do nicely.

Alexander was quite satisfied with these arrangements. We collect students' fees in, say, pounds. We forward two-thirds of these to Alexander who pays rent, teachers and Russian housewives. The executives commented on the high quality of the teaching and food. Up to now we have never had a hiccup.

ANTONINA'S VACUUM CLEANERS

Antonina remained very much on the periphery of these negotiations, though she certainly took good care of me personally while I was in Volgograd. The temperature was minus 20 degrees and a bitingly cold easterly whistled in every morning from the steppes and over the frozen Caspian. It was good to have well-heeled friends with a warm flat, though I could not complain about Eisenhower's bed. The caretaker served the same breakfast every morning – champagne and caviar on toast. I thought at first that he was trying to impress me, but Alexander explained to me that such things were easy to come by. Champagne – of the Russian variety – is not expensive and does not taste too bad. Caviar comes from that region – the Caspian Sea and the river itself. All caviar is the property of the state, and there are severe penalties for fishermen who do not turn over the sturgeons they catch to the local authorities. However, human nature is human nature, and at that time the 'authorities' were in pretty bad shape. Alexander showed me a photo, taken by a fishing friend, of a sturgeon which had been opened up to reveal 20 kilos of caviar in its ample stomach.

My Russian friends showed me Volgograd. In spite of the freezing conditions, I managed to get about quite a lot, though sights worth seeing are few, since the town was blown to pieces in the prolonged struggle with the Germans. The buildings are consequently post-war – ponderous square and oblong blocs thrown up by unimaginative Soviet constructors. The town possesses, however, one of the largest statues in the world – *The Motherland Calls* – a huge bronze effigy of a very Slavic lady looking down from the heights over the broad Volga. It is very impressive, either in spite of or because of its sheer bulk, and expresses the strong bonds that most Russians feel for their homeland.

Worth seeing, too, is the Museum of the Battle of Stalingrad. Murals occupy 360 degrees of wall space – one can get quite dizzy spinning round to take it all in. The various stages of the battle are vividly depicted in striking colour. The message is, of course, a little one-sided, but the artistry is commendable and conveys clearly the suffering, bravery and sheer desperation of the soldiers and civilians involved in this momentous and bitter struggle.

Antonina's husband, Boris, ran a sizeable factory producing industrial components of some kind. He was the prototypical Russian – hearty, boisterous, hospitable – had a great moustache and spoke no English. It was clear, however, that Antonina was the powerful one. The good quality of their clothes and the warmth and opulent furnishing of their flat left you in no doubt as to the considerable resources that the family possessed. I asked Alexander where the wealth had come from. Again, the situation was very Russian, at least typical of the particular transition in which Russia found itself at the time.

Antonina had been very active in the local Communist Party and had gradually worked her way up the system, eventually becoming one of the movers and shakers in the local council. This position did not bring any money in itself, but officials latch on to certain privileges, not uncommon in a variety of regimes. One day, in the Brezhnev era, Antonina was made responsible for the distribution of 150 vacuum cleaners of surprisingly good quality to the citizens of Volgograd. Anyone familiar with the workings of the Soviet system will know that goods tend to become available in large batches after perhaps many months or even years of scarcity. They are then distributed, in some weird fashion, in Soviet townships whereupon they are immediately gobbled up by a starved public with millions of unused roubles in the bank. The cost of the article, officially fixed at a low level by the command economy, presents no problem. How to get your hands on it is the trick.

Volgograd had a population of well over a million, so that 150 vacuum cleaners would not go very far. Antonina suddenly acquired many friends and admirers with dusty floors. Who would get the machines? The first personage to get one was the Rector of Volgograd University, into which one of Antonina's daughters had been trying to get for some time. Other citizens who had an influence on the procurement of cars, building sites or machinery or who had access to special avenues of political influence, also became vacuum cleaner families. By cunning and very leisurely bartering, Antonina joined the class of new Russian millionaires. Some of her wealth she may have used to become a Member of Parliament. Boris got his factory.

The Zhilins were very generous and kind-hearted hosts. There was no way you could obviate the five-floor climb up the concrete stairway of their apartment block (in the dark after 7pm), for Soviet architects put in lifts only if buildings had six floors or more, but once in their homes nothing was denied to a Zhilin guest. Their furniture, household appliances and gleaming American-style kitchen were reminiscent of what we imagine graced the dachas of Khrushchev, Brezhnev, Gorbachev and their buddies. Dinner was delicious. Even the conversation, conducted largely by virtue of the fluent English of the two attractive, university-educated and elegantly attired Zhilin daughters, was nothing less than sparkling. Russians, often curt and brusque in public on account of their unfortunate and oppressive history, are openly benign and engaging in their own homes.

The following summer Antonina and Boris came to Riversdown for a month-long English course each. She, with her outgoing personality, learned a tremendous amount. Boris absorbed a bit less, but enjoyed himself, while his steppe masculinity and handsomeness allied to his unfailing joviality compensated for the occasional shakiness of his embryonic grammar. The Zhilins transferred to the bank £20,000 more than the amount corresponding to their fees. This they blew in one and a half hours in an Edinburgh fashion shop, to the considerable annoyance of Mrs Nakanishi, wife of a Japanese billionaire, who, on accompanying them on their shopping expedition, felt obliged to spend £25,000 so as not to be outdone.

35

THE BERLITZ FAMILY

The most famous language teaching organization in the world was, and probably still is, the Berlitz School of Languages. There are about 200 Berlitz schools in the world in more than 50 countries. As it is one of the oldest language teaching chains in the world – it was founded in 1878 – there are many amusing anecdotes of a cross-cultural nature that are worth retelling. One of them concerns Berlitz activities during the Second World War.

Maximilian D. Berlitz was not, as is often believed, a German. He was an Alsatian Frenchman who emigrated to Rhode Island in the United States and opened the first school there in 1878 to teach French to Americans. His method was so successful that it was subsequently adapted to teach English, Spanish, German and most other languages. It is often described as the Direct Method, as the teacher uses only the target language from the very beginning and prohibits entirely the student's own tongue during instruction and conversation. If you imagine yourself learning Lithuanian or Tibetan without a word of explanation in your own or any other common language, you may envisage a situation where difficulty, misunderstanding, even incomprehension would reign. This is not, however, the case. Once the student has survived the initial shock of being addressed in Tibetan and has perceived that he actually understands, the resulting gain in confidence enables him to deal directly with the language instead of discussing it for hours in another.

Everything naturally depends on the skill of the teacher in correctly perceiving and then adhering to the almost foolproof progression of vocabulary items and grammatical structures that Maximilian Berlitz had so painstakingly worked out. In my experience, only about 10 per cent of language teachers are able to do this, though the approach is not difficult to learn, provided that the teacher himself is properly trained. It takes 100 hours of theory and practice – mainly the latter – under the guidance of an expert. Then you can do it for the rest of your life. Most new teachers are subjected to hurried or inadequate training and emerge from their method course 'half-baked' and somewhat confused. Their confusion is small compared to that which they will shortly impart to their students. A competent Direct Method instructor, on the other hand, can give his student oral fluency and a working knowledge of any language in a few weeks.

Between 1955 and 1971 I opened franchises for Berlitz, founding the organization in Finland, Norway and Portugal and running schools for them in London. Later I founded Berlitz East Asia, headquartered in Tokyo. In this context I became acquainted with more than a hundred school directors in Europe and another 50 or so in the United States (the Americans owned the rights to Japan). In 1966 I toured the Berlitz Schools of America; there were considerable differences between the schools of the United States and Europe. Even more pronounced was the difference between European and American directors. The latter were a well-trained team of sales-oriented, profit-minded executives; the former a mostly academic, old-fashioned genteel family of sentimentalists who sometimes made money and at other times did not.

Most of the European directors, like old Berlitz himself, were genteel, often absent-minded linguists whose schools constituted an integral part of their lives. It was indeed a lifestyle in itself. The Berlitz director in Bologna or Berlin had been around for years, his father and mother for a generation before that. Several government ministers, perhaps a prince or two, had studied French, Italian or Russian under his tutelage, and the local barons of industry entrusted to him their 14-year-old sons. His wife gave teas for ladies of society; if the school made money, they perhaps owned a modest villa in Antibes or Benidorm (then unspoiled), and once every summer a fleet of hired coaches would take the entire body of students out to a splendid picnic in the Vienna Woods, the Tuscan hills or the Bois de Vincennes. Some of these men had written books, which did not sell very well, and more than one had published collections of poems. Every four years this gracefully ageing generation celebrated another *étape* of Berlitz existence at the *Congrès*, to which they flocked in new clothes and old cars – many Rovers and Citroëns, not a few stately Mercedes and Lancias, and at least one black-and-yellow Rolls-Royce.

In the United States the Berlitz organization was a well-oiled machine that made money. This is not to say that it did not adhere faithfully to the worthy principles that had served as a basis for worldwide success. In many respects Berlitz teaching in America was more thorough, conscientiously applied and certainly more rigorously monitored than was instruction in Europe. The difference was that in the United States everything was on a strict business basis, as opposed to the European style of pursuing a life's hobby, and hopefully getting paid for it.

In Europe one discussed the students' wishes and needs, the twists and idiosyncrasies of the target language, a mutually convenient timetable and selection of teachers, a suitable break in instruction to accommodate holidays and family weddings – rarely did one talk about money or dates for payment. One sent a bill, after a decent interval, to the company, the parent, the ministry or the Palace. In America it was cash up front, as much of it as possible, please. One did not sell lessons 20 or 30 at a time, one sold them in hundreds, maybe a thousand, if Chinese or Tibetan was required. I cannot sell you 50 lessons, Madam, you have to buy 200 – that way you make a commitment to learn the language. If you have paid for these lessons in advance, you will take them and you will learn. We cannot afford failures, Madam, we have a reputation to protect.

During the Second World War, the Nazis occupied a large part of Europe including those countries where the large majority of Berlitz schools were located. The headquarters of the Société internationale des écoles Berlitz were housed in 31 boulevard des Italians in Paris, and it was here that Berlitz policy was directed, new franchises were granted and, most importantly, royalties were collected. As in most French organizations, centralization of control was a primary objective and, though the Berlitz empire was spread over a motley collection of nations, Paris was able, in the main, to keep tabs on their disparate subjects and maintain a respectable degree of uniformity and fiscal benefit.

It was obvious that the Germans would seek to control all educational institutions in France as elsewhere, and indeed Europe's Berlitz schools, while being allowed to continue their activity, gradually became part of the training facilities of the Third Reich. In order, however, to protect the theoretical autonomy of the Société internationale des écoles Berlitz, not to mention its financial resources and royalty-collecting privileges, the headquarters of the Société was moved, for the duration of hostilities, to the country most likely to remain out of the Nazi clutches – Britain.

The director of the London Berlitz school in 1940 was a middle-aged retired army officer, John Gilbert. Gilbert – one of those forthright, no-nonsense Englishmen instrumental in building the Empire – was aided in his duties by his former batman and devoted disciple, William Myers, slightly younger than his commander. When Gilbert was approached by Paris on the subject of transferring the Berlitz headquarters, he unhesitatingly shouldered the burden, on condition that the London school should remain his property not only for the duration of the war, but during the rest of his lifetime and should be passed on to Myers for as long as he lived, too. Such was the loyalty and faith between brother exofficers. Paris, though reluctant to hand over the sizeable company-owned London school, had no option but to comply and the contract was signed.

Few European royalties were paid to London during the years 1940–45, though Spain contributed the odd amount and there were some touching instances of faithful German concessionaires trying to maintain tenuous contact with the Société. Many French Berlitzers wound up as prisoners of war, in German concentration camps. One of them, a middle-aged director called Durand, had a most uncomfortable experience one winter's day when the prisoners, as part of a disciplinary measure, were forced to lie face downwards on the wet ground and be harangued, in this supine posture, by the camp commandant. To make matters worse, a new adjutant to the commandant strode up and down among the prostrated Frenchmen and eventually put his foot on the back of poor Durand's head. As he pressed the Berlitz man's face into the mud, he whispered into his ear:

'It's Schneider here. Berlitz Karlsruhe. Don't worry, everything's going to be OK. I'm moving you to a better block – the warmest – and I have a couple of big food parcels for you, as well as cigarettes and cognac. See you in church.'

STAGNARO

Paris Berlitz was more than just a school. It had occupied its building – Palais Berlitz – for many decades. It contained a cinema of the same name and, of course, Café Berlitz, which did a roaring trade resuscitating shattered Americans after two or three hours' immersion in French. The school's strategic location on the boulevards, its large and variegated student body and its continuous record of instruction since the end of the nineteenth century lent it an old-world, cosmopolitan atmosphere which the introduction of 'modern methods' entirely failed to dispel.

This venerable institution had its many legends and annals, which included the tantrums of famous film stars, scandalous romances among eminent figures of society, comings and goings of princes and princesses with their bodyguards, fabulous sums spent on lessons by American millionaires and a host of other minor excitements which seemed to occur every week. In the fortnight our training group spent there, we were not disappointed.

Berlitz, after a long period of agonizing, had finally invested in some language laboratory equipment. As the shape of the building did not lend itself to the creation of a large actual laboratory, Montfort had had installed, in the quieter back part of the school, half a dozen small, individual booths where students could don their earphones and listen to their tapes undisturbed. Each booth was curtained off to ensure privacy.

In a school the size of the one in Paris, one always needs a handyman; since the advent of electronic equipment, it had become important that this person had the capability of keeping the lab in good shape and fixing broken machines when necessary. Luciano Stagnaro was such a man. A dark-skinned, gnarled Sicilian of middle age, he resembled a Mediterranean goatherd more than an electrician, but he came cheap, was devoted to the school and prowled the dark corridors 10 hours a day.

The Paris Berlitz school was a large triangular building on the boulevard des Italiens, a stone's throw from the Opéra. The isosceles triangle was divided into many rooms – reception and administration being located at the front on the short side of the triangle and about 60 classrooms extending back along the other two sides. One entered the school through a well-lit area which served as reception, waiting room and general rendezvous point for students and teachers finding each other before or between lessons. Departing students would often hang around here to discuss their experiences, pay their bills and briefly socialize. Classrooms were aligned along the sides of the triangle, the language lab booths being furthest from reception. To inspect the school, you went round the triangle, returning to your starting point in due course: there was no other way out. The cashier was strategically placed closest to the exit.

One morning as we underwent our training in one of the bigger classrooms, an intruder made his way into the school. This was not difficult, as in midmorning the reception area was thronged, and his arrival went unnoticed. We did not learn much about him except that he was French, fairly well dressed and was a sex pest. After some time, he discovered the language booths, peered through the curtains and found a young, blonde Californian girl in deep concentration on her exercises. He tried to assault her. You can well imagine the effect of the student's screams as she struggled to free herself.

Stagnaro (I believe the name means 'pond-minder') heard them first, as he was not far from his precious booths. He ran to the scene, whipping open the curtains of each one till he found the intruder. The latter, after one look at Stagnaro's craggy weatherbeaten features, abandoned his Californian prey, smashed his way past the hesitating Sicilian and ran pell-mell down one of the long corridors of the isosceles triangle. Stagnaro, recovering quickly, went off in hot pursuit, screaming fearsome oaths in Corleone Sicilian.

The fugitive reached the reception area, which was packed with students and Berlitz staff. What this body of people saw was a well-dressed Frenchman, looking fearful in the extreme, being desperately chased by a mean-looking stubbly-chinned, rampageous hobo screeching hysterically in a weird cacophonous tongue. Two sizeable Americans, men of action as they were, quickly took in the scene and jumped on Stagnaro, pinning him to the floor. Other students piled in to help immobilize the Sicilian while a French student ran outside to find a gendarme. The sex maniac, given a moment's respite, was nevertheless unable to force his way through the thronged exit, so he ran into an adjacent office and jumped· through the window, cutting himself seriously in the process. He then fled across the busy boulevard des ltaliens and disappeared down a side street.

After some frantic explanations on the part of the Berlitz office staff, the American Good Samaritans reluctantly released Stagnaro, by now frothing at the mouth and about to be arrested by the newly arrived gendarme, who felt he had to start taking notes, instead of chasing the fugitive.

It appeared that the intruder had made good his escape, but it was not to be. When the police eventually initiated pursuit, their task was easy, as the badly cut miscreant left a trail of blood right across the boulevard and down several side streets. As they followed the gory tracks, the amount of blood increased until finally, after 1 kilometre, they came to a veritable pool of blood where the Frenchman had lain, now unconscious, for 20 minutes. Back at school the Americans took Stagnaro out for a couple of stiff drinks – he liked grappa – though he normally abstained till seven in the evening.

LASSE VIRÉN'S LIFE STORY

Lasse Virén is considered by many to be the greatest long-distance runner of modern times. Following in the footsteps of his illustrious famous compatriots, Paavo Nurmi and Ville Ritola (two Finns who dominated all track events from 800 metres to the marathon in Olympics between the two world wars), Lasse, emerging at the last moment as a contestant, won the 5000 metres and 10,000 metres events in the Munich Olympic Games in 1972 and repeated the feat in Montreal in 1976.

Lasse was born in the small village of Myrskylä in south-eastern Finland. Before taking up running, he worked for his family's firm driving lorries in the surrounding rural areas. At different times in his life, he was a policeman and, after achieving fame, a Member of Parliament. In the 1990s I got to know Lasse well, and he and his wife, Païvi, often went sailing with us. He is a man who takes pride in doing things well. Though an inexperienced sailor, he quickly adapted to life on board, raising sails, working the winches, steering when required. Our skippers, loving his industrious nature, entrusted him with as many on-deck tasks as he could handle. Though extremely shy and taciturn, even by Finnish standards, Lasse later learned to make creditable speeches even in front of seasoned politicians.

The day came when it was important for Lasse to improve his English language skills, hitherto acquired sporadically on sports tracks and in changing rooms in the numerous countries where he had competed. I recommended he come to study at Riversdown House. Lasse came for three weeks, one-to-one instruction, and improved his English steadily. To the delight of the other dozen or so international students, he went for a 8-kilometre run every morning and some of the braver, or younger, ones tried to follow him. They could not stay with him, of course, but it served to get them out of bed in the morning.

At the end of their course, all Riversdown students are asked to make a presentation, usually about their company. Those from multinational firms did this eagerly. Those students who are not working for companies are given an essay to do instead.

Usually they are asked to write their life story. Lasse was given this task. Working at it for two days he eventually produced a seven-page essay describing the life of Lasse Virén.

His main teacher took great interest in reading and correcting his essay – it was quite detailed, with fairly good grammar, and his teacher was pleased with his progress. I asked her how she judged the essay.

'Very creditable,' she replied, 'and quite interesting. Only one funny thing, though . . .'

'What was that?' I asked.

'He never mentioned running.'

MAANINKA

The 1980 Olympic Games were held in Moscow. For political reasons, they were boycotted by the United States, but the rest of the world showed up. In the absence of the Americans, the British team did very well in the field events, Sebastian Coe and Steve Ovett winning gold medals.

I was interested in the performance of Lasse Virén, who had won successive gold medals in the Munich and Montreal Games. He was not expected to win in Moscow in view of his age and powerful Ethiopian opposition but had agreed to participate in the 10,000 metres to support another Finn – Kaarlo Maaninka – who had a chance of a medal.

At the time we employed a Finnish live-in au pair, whom I invited to join us to watch the 10,000 metres event on television. She was from Lapland and possessed the extremely reticent characteristics of individuals from that Arctic region. She appeared unmoved by a series of rather exciting races leading up to the 10,000 metres, sitting impassively in a corner of our sitting room, neither smiling nor scowling, ignoring our lively reactions to the events on the screen. Nevertheless, though motionless and expressionless, she watched intently.

The 10,000 metres unfolded dramatically. The two Ethiopians, Yifter and his backup, led most of the laps, with Virén and Maaninka in hot pursuit. The positions remained unchanged until four laps from the end when Virén surged into the lead and forced Yifter and his colleague to up their pace in order not to lose him. Our au pair showed no emotion whatsoever, though we were jumping up and down on our seats. Viren's sprint was obviously a tactical manoeuvre – Yifter was the overwhelming favourite. He had an irresistible sprint finish, and Lasse was trying to take the sting out of this before the final lap. He was partly successful inasmuch as Yifter had to step up his pace earlier than he wanted to and the second Ethiopian lost his plan and was passed by Maaninka, who was running strongly. Still Marja sat mutely in the corner.

Two laps from the end, Virén had played his part. He dropped back and let Maaninka pass him to chase Yifter. The second Ethiopian was no longer in contention for gold or silver. As Yifter went hell for leather, Maaninka accelerated in turn and manfully chased the speedy African. With one lap to go, Marja suddenly leapt out of her corner, scuttled across to the television and screamed in Finnish 'Mene, Kaarlo, mene, Kaarlo!' (Go, Kaarlo, go, go, go!) During the minute and a half that the final lap lasted, Marja jumped up and down in front of the TV, screeched like I have never heard a Finn screech before, flailed her arms round like a windmill and collapsed in perspiring exhaustion as Maaninka crossed the line for a silver medal.

When she had recovered sufficiently to speak, I said to her, 'Marja, I never saw you so excited – what got into you?'

'Maaninka's my brother!' she screamed at me.

ESTONIAN SOCCER RIOT

The story that follows is one of two where I attempt to show how one can get a false impression of a country when entering it for the first time.

A young English teacher, Stanley Shaw, had just arrived in Helsinki to teach for a year in our school. We had secured a nice flat for him near his place of work, and I accompanied him to open it up and show him round. He was pleased to find Finnish apartments spacious, airy and well equipped. This one had a nice view of a bit of forest. As he unpacked his luggage and put his clothes into the cupboards, I checked the lamps, gas, electricity and so on. Finally, I tried the television. I found I had switched on a black-and-white Estonian channel and was about to change it when Shaw exclaimed enthusiastically, 'Great! Football! Can I watch it?'

Slightly irritated at having my routine tour disturbed, I never-theless relented: he was a keen sportsman, as I like to think myself to be. I decided to stay with him half an hour to watch the match. It was boring in the extreme, but Shaw enthused over every pass. It was in the Soviet era, and Tallinn, the Estonian club side, was playing at home against a lowly Russian team from just over the border. The football was of poor quality; the only items of interest were the rough tackling and the constant fouling on both sides. Finally, after a violent Estonian foul, the referee, who was Russian, awarded a penalty to the Russian visitors. The Estonian crowd erupted; as the Russian penalty-taker lined up for the spot kick, some of the spectators began to climb over the barriers. When he scored, making the score 2–1 in the Russian team's favour, the entire crowd invaded the pitch. An irate spectator knocked the referee to the ground.

The Russian team members, coming to the ref's aid, were subsequently attacked by the Estonian players, aided and abetted by the Estonian spectators. The referee, helped to his feet, promptly fled the pitch, accompanied by his two linesmen. Minutes later, riot police, emerging from half a dozen buses stationed outside the stadium, rushed on to the pitch and used batons on defiant spectators. The latter, enraged at the prospect of Estonian police beating Estonian compatriots, regrouped, tore up stadium seats and hurled themselves at the policemen. The battle raged for a quarter of an hour, with the crowd beginning to gain the upper hand by virtue of their superior numbers and improvised weapons. The police formed a tight group behind protective shields and edged slowly towards the stadium exit. The two teams had started their own fist fight in one of the goalmouths.

At the height of this mayhem and with the flight of the police seeming imminent, the fire brigade arrived – apparently a special unit – and turned four powerful water hoses on to the front line of spectators. Those were forced gradually to retreat, especially when the police were reinforced with tear gas bombs. After 45 minutes of battle, subjected to chemical and hosepipe attack, the crowd began to look a little worse for wear and slowly were channelled to an escape route via the stadium rear entrance, screaming abuse at the officials all the while. It was a full hour before the stadium was cleared of belligerents, some of whom refused to submit and were consequently manhandled, arrested and bundled into three police vans which had pulled up alongside the pitch, now extensively littered with remnants of seats, broken bottles and the occasional prostrate body. The stadium lights were doused, the gates locked, the show was over.

Shaw gaped at me.

'Are all Finnish football matches like this?' he asked.

'Every Saturday,' I replied cruelly.

He learned the truth the next day, but I could not miss the chance to delude him.

THE BEAUTIFUL NAMES OF ALLAH

In the 1980s I supervised an intensive English language course for six Arabs from Abu Dhabi. Five of them were adults in their twenties and thirties. One was a boy of 15 – an outstanding student, but wilful and undisciplined. He persistently played truant from class, and, in view of his age, I became worried about his safety. After several warnings, I gave him a stern dressing-down one morning in front of the others and told him one more truancy would result in his being packed off back to Abu Dhabi on the morrow. My action had the desired effect. After that he attended all classes and learned a lot of English, though I did not get another friendly look or word from him for the rest of the month. He left scowling.

Fifteen years passed. One day my telephone rang, and a firm of English contractors asked for me. I had had no previous contact with them, but they were doing big business in Abu Dhabi and English instruction needed organizing for 200 trainees in that country. Their contract was with ADNOC – the Abu Dhabi National Oil Company – by far the richest firm in a very rich country. The director of ADNOC, who felt personally involved in the ambitious training scheme (two years), had insisted that it must be organized by me. I asked who my unknown backer might be. His name was Abdullah al-Badi, one of the most affluent and influential figures in the kingdom.

Apparently, he had known me as a 15-year-old, not long after he had lost his father, and had so much appreciated the 'parental care' bestowed on him that he wished to recognize it in the current situation.

Some weeks later I went out to the Emirates and did the job for Abdullah, now a charming, fiercely energetic and successful executive, as well as a good husband, caring father and breeder of some of the fastest camels in the Gulf. Only the Maktoum family beats the al-Badis in the Dubai classic camel races, which I attended with my former pupil. We have remained firm friends ever since. Abdullah – intelligent, conscientious, loyal, and of impeccable manners and morals – is a splendid representative of his part of the world.

The second time I went to Abu Dhabi I shared an unusual and memorable occasion with him. The al-Badi family own several fine houses in the old capital of Abu Dhabi, AI Ain, which is situated in the middle of the desert, not far from the frontier of Oman. Abdullah invited me to stay there overnight and see some of the desert in the process.

Like many sheikhs, he drove a Mercedes, and he had just taken possession of a brand-new scarlet 560. In this we streaked along the excellent road to AI Ain, he and I in the front and a huge bodyguard called Ali in the back. I have always been interested in the Islamic religion and the way in which it shapes the behaviour of its adherents. Abdullah, on several occasions, was kind enough to explain the various precepts of Islam, which, in many ways, are strikingly similar to those of Christianity. Abdullah, a devout believer, has great didactic talent, and he succeeded in imparting to me the depth of feeling, sincerity and conviction that religious practice inspired in him. On the way to AI Ain he developed the theme once more.

About halfway through the journey he drove off the tarmac surface of the high road, going off at a tangent across the firm, flat sands. In about half an hour, close to a picturesque escarpment, we came across a camel farm, which he owned. We spent an hour inspecting the fine animals – they had impressive pedigrees and were bred to win races in Dubai. There were some lovable baby camels. Abdullah told me how much they were worth – I remember there were a lot of zeroes in the figures. Around five o'clock he and the bodyguard climbed 50 metres or so up the escarpment, knelt down facing Mecca and prayed, while I took pictures of the animals.

Abdullah said goodbye to the camel keepers (they seemed devoted to him) and informed me that we were now in a bit of a hurry, as dinner awaited us at his brother's home in AI Ain. As his brother, General Mohammed al-Badi, was the Abu Dhabi Chief of Staff, more punctuality was required than is usual around those parts. Abdullah explained to me that, instead of returning to the high road, he would drive as the crow flies, straight across the desert. The sand was hard for 30 kilometres but might get a bit softer after that. In any case, I was not to worry – it was quite safe.

We fastened our seat belts and took off on screeching tyres and flying sand. I am used to Stags and Jaguars myself, but I can tell you that a 560 pushed almost to the limit by a race-minded young Arab with no traffic to worry about takes a lot of catching, if by any chance you want to catch it. Sand spurted 2 metres high from our rear wheels as we poured the desert in front of us down our radiator at 220 kilometres an hour. When we got to the softer sand the plumes on either side behind us rose to a height of 10 to 12 metres at least and must, like the pyramids, have been visible from space.

The sun turned crimson and, as sunset approached, Abdullah asked me if I would mind if he went through the Beautiful Names of Allah ritual. I had heard of this custom but never experienced it from close up. It is believed that Allah has 99 names, and recounting these names is a form of ritual prayer. To my surprise, Abdullah began to intone the prayer at the top of his voice, and his decibel count offered valiant competition with both the sound of the accelerating Mercedes 12-cylinder engine doing 250 kilometres per hour and the resoundingly sibilant hiss of the twin plumes of sand being projected heavenwards.

As the magnificent sun dipped below the horizon, the desert took on hues of indigo and gold and Abdullah switched on his powerful headlights, illuminating large turquoise cacti and scattering small desert creatures. I was overtaken by a sense of exhilaration engendered by the magic of the evening sky, the emerging stars, the impassioned prayer and the sheer speed across the empty stretches. It was a driver's paradise – no speed limits, no policemen, no traffic or traffic lights, no annoying intersections, no road in fact. For me it was a once-in-a-lifetime experience, and I can only admire Abdullah, fine driver as he is, who got all three of us alive to Al Ain and in time for supper.

41

CAMEL-BOYS IN HUDDERSFIELD

A special case arose in the summer of 1978, when a British company from Huddersfield ran into problems in Libya. This firm sold sewage works to various overseas entities and had contracted with the Libyan government to set up a huge sewage plant near Benghazi. The normal procedure was to send out a dozen Yorkshire engineers to see to the building of the plant, to supervise the first six months of its operation and to train about 60 local staff for its future maintenance. Communication was obviously a problem, but the Yorkshiremen had managed fairly well in some countries where French or Spanish was spoken or where there was a reasonable level of English among the locals.

In Libya the difficulties of communication were compounded by several cultural and linguistic factors. In the first place, people living in oil-rich states had got used to the idea of never doing any manual work or menial labour of any kind. The activities to be carried out at sewage plants entailed no small amount of drudgery, while the olfactory ambience left much to be desired. It proved therefore impossible for the Libyans to recruit staff from cities such as Benghazi or Tripoli, where a certain level of pseudo-sophistication had been adopted by urban dwellers. In fact, the only men they could find to do the job were 60 camel-boys from the desert. They did not have urban pretensions and were used to dealing with large piles of camel dung.

I have to tell you, dear reader, that Libyan camel-boys aged 16–19 who have spent all their short lives in the desert, who know little of city life or even the terms to describe it, who can barely read or write their own language (Arabic) and who have never experienced contact with a foreigner or a foreign tongue, hardly represent the cream of the cream when it comes to learning English. Even the Arabic they spoke was a relatively obscure Bedouin dialect not fully understood by Benghazi clerics, so that matching up this language gem with Huddersfield English was clearly going to be no piece of cake.

It might have been easier to teach 10 Yorkshiremen Arabic, but after a few weeks out there the engineers from the Pennines strongly refused to undertake the task. It would have taken a long time, they would not even speak real Arabic at the end of it and . . . they hated the place. The company bit the bullet and asked us to organize instruction for the camel-boys. They had thought at first of a summer course, but two months (the period the colleges were free) was clearly too short a time to achieve any result. We set up a six-month course to be given in rented premises in Huddersfield.

I will not go into all the details of the Yorkshire sojourn of these young Libyans. Suffice it to say that their studies were punctuated by episodes of shoplifting, student strikes, fires lit in metal wastepaper baskets in their bedrooms, endemic truancy and, in many cases, zero progress in their learning. Teetotallers at home, they indulged in the offerings of the local pubs, often collapsed on their beds fully dressed, and not infrequently had to be dragged out of bed at noon to attend their lessons. Good bacon-and-egg breakfasts were of no use to them (Muslims don't eat pork); many of them had little experience of eating vegetables, either.

Well, in the end it wasn't so bad. About one-third of them learned to communicate in Huddersfield English and, in due course, this helped to set up the plant (a little behind schedule). Nobody starved to death or jumped out of a window, though with some of our teachers and landladies it was a near thing.

The poor boys themselves were in no way to blame. The episode only serves to show that, in many instances, cultural barriers often outweigh linguistic ones during the acquisition of a second tongue.

42

FIGHTING HARADA

At the end of the 1960s, a Japanese boxer named Fighting Harada was featherweight champion of the world. Not many Japanese fighters achieve this rank, and my friend Komine was a great fan of his. One night in June, Harada was called upon to defend his world title against a dangerous Mexican called Hernández. Komine came over to the Asia Center where I was staying in Tokyo and asked me to watch the fight with him on TV. We ordered sandwiches and installed ourselves comfortably among a motley crowd of males from different countries in the lounge of the Center.

The fighters were evenly matched. Harada clearly won the first round, Hernández the second. The Japanese champion dominated the next three rounds, but the Mexican refused to tire and probably took rounds 6, 7 and 8. Komine, normally a calm individual, kept jumping up and down like he was sitting on hot coals. In those days world boxing championship finals were decided over 15 rounds; consequently, boxers needed considerable stamina and powers of endurance; the last five rounds usually developed into a rather bloody spectacle.

I was kind of supporting Harada, partly for Komine's sake and partly on account of my admiration for the Japanese sense of fair play. The honourable Harada, however, took quite a beating from the doughty Mexican during rounds 9 to 13, and

CLOSE ENCOUNTERS OF A CULTURAL KIND

even a spirited rally by Fighting in the 14th round smacked of too little too late. Harada was nevertheless renowned for his fighting finishes, so I still clung to a faint hope that he might triumph.

At the end of the 14th round, Komine excused himself and hurried from the room. I supposed he was availing himself of the one-minute pause between rounds to visit the toilet – he had been practically peeing in his pants since round 6. He had not reappeared when the bell rang for the final round, so I stopped looking for him and concentrated on the fight. It was thrilling in the extreme.

Harada could not face the sense of shame that a defeat in front of his home crowd would entail; he dug deep into his last reserves of strength, courage and ferocity and got right on top of Hernández, who was lucky to stay on his weary feet at the end. The boxers retired to their corners and there was some delay until the referee summoned them to the centre of the ring and announced Fighting Harada still champion of the world. The audience cheered.

Komine re-entered the lounge and came straight to me.

'Who won?' he asked anxiously. I told him the result; he seemed quite relieved.

'Why on earth didn't you stay to see the last round?' I asked.

'I couldn't stand the tension,' said Komine.

43

THE KINGS COURT HOTEL

In order to secure accommodation at a reasonable price in London every summer (the months of June, July and August always produced a student 'bulge') I had been negotiating a special tariff with this hotel based on guaranteed numbers each summer for the next two or three years. The Kings Court Hotel was a pleasant little two-star establishment in Bayswater, unpretentious in the extreme, but conveniently located for shopping and sightseeing and not too far from our South Audley Street school. The then owner, a gentleman from the south of France named Crespo, told me about some of the problems he had encountered when he had purchased the property the previous year. The building had been in a general state of disrepair and the key employee, around whom the events of each day seemed to revolve, was an ageing caretaker named Simm.

Crespo took over the management himself, but he noticed that the reception staff, chambermaids, waiters and kitchen staff always checked with Simm before they did anything. The hotel was unremarkable as far as the reception and bedrooms were concerned, its only notable feature being a fine, square dining room with a huge, multi-panelled window (occupying virtually the whole wall) at one end. One stuffy evening, Crespo asked one of the waiters to open the central section of this fine window to let in a little air for the guests. The waiter protested that the window had never been opened during the years he had been employed by the hotel and ignored Crespo's exhortations to open it until Simm was sent for.

When the septuagenarian caretaker arrived, his face also registered horror at Crespo's proposal, and he swore the window had not been opened for 30 years. Crespo was, however, a true son of the Midi and was not to be disobeyed. He forced Simm to go through with it. The latter fetched a ladder and, climbing up it, tugged with all his strength at the catch on the central panel. Nothing happened for a minute or so, then suddenly, on further exhortation from Crespo, Simm, with a superhuman tug, flew backwards from his ladder and brought the whole window (i.e. the wall) down into the dining room. Diners were cut by flying glass, one of the waitresses had to be treated for shock, and Simm was taken to hospital with concussion.

The new window cost Crespo the year's forecasted profit; his increasing irritation with Simm led him to fire the caretaker against the earnest advice of the entire staff. The problem seemed to be the cellar, where the controls for water, gas and electricity were located and where only Simm had operated for more than two decades. The cellar was criss-crossed with wires to such an extent that one could not cross from one side to the other without twisting, turning, bending and contorting oneself in a manner which only Simm seemed able to handle. On the morning after he was fired, Crespo went down to the cellar with a young electrician and spent a few hours rearranging the maze of wires in a more rational and orderly fashion. After that nothing in the hotel worked properly. Toilets flushed with hot water; emergency lighting woke everybody up in the middle of the night, arid the fire alarm went off three times a day. The cellar had to be 'redone' at further great expense.

In order to meet his rising repair bills, Crespo lowered his room charges to attract a greater number of guests. He had little success, so he lowered them even further. Eventually the advantageous prices attracted customers from two organizations – the Women's Church Guilds and the US Army. The Church Guilds had frequent conferences in London and, being short of cash, were desperate for low-cost accommodation for visiting delegates from the provinces. American soldiers, on a few days' leave in the English capital, were also on the lookout for cheap rooms. For a while Crespo filled his hotel.

The ensuing problem was what one today might call client synergy, or more exactly, room use. The American soldiers would have parties in the middle of the night and stagger round the corridors from room to room, often in a drunken stupor. Church Guildswomen on the way to the bathroom might be grabbed by a myopic corporal or confronted by a naked call girl. Sometimes the soldiers burst into the Guildswomen's rooms (by mistake). Crespo rarely slept. Eventually he banned all US soldiers, but the Church Guilds opted for alternative accommodation and Kings Court found peace again.

By the time Crespo had found us, he had completed his repairs, mended the hotel's reputation and slightly raised his prices. We used the hotel for several summers and never had a serious problem with the establishment. I recount these events, as Crespo related them to me, to give an example of the lack of professionalism I encountered in many instances in dealing with British firms in those years. I am English and happy to be so, but as it was the first time I had worked in an English business environment, I could not help but feel that Britain was being passed, in terms of efficiency, clear goals and modern approach, not only by the Americans, Germans and Scandinavians, but possibly by the French and others as well.

FACING TURBULENCE

My friend Michael Gates took a Lufthansa flight from Frankfurt to the United States. Most of the passengers were Germans or Americans. In the middle of the Atlantic, the aircraft began to encounter turbulence. As it increased, the German pilot felt duty bound to inform the passengers of the situation and calm their fears. He made two announcements – one in German and the second in American English. The German announcement translated roughly as follows:

'As you can see, we have encountered very high turbulence. This has been caused by wind speeds of up to 137 kilometres per hour. But there is no need to worry, as this plane is built to very high engineering standards and able to withstand a G-force of 2.5 and has four powerful 373-kilonewton General Electric engines [at which point the US passengers – having understood only the words 'General Electric' – looked worried]. What I intend to do to counter this is to descend by 7000 feet. The reason for this is that we are likely to find lower and steadier wind speeds at that level. If that doesn't work, don't worry, as I am sure we will be able to find a level less affected, and there are fewer reports of turbulence as we approach Boston, which we should do in around 27 minutes.'

Conscious of addressing a different audience, the pilot, speaking in perfect US English, drawled to the Americans:

'As you can see, we are on a bit of a roller coaster. So just sit back, tighten your seatbelts, and enjoy the ride!'

THE GERMAN MODEL

In the late 1990s, I was asked to go to Hungary to deliver a three-day seminar to a group of German and Hungarian executives. Deutsche Telekom had purchased a controlling share of Matáv, the Hungarian telephone company. A culture clash was inevitable, and it was resolved to hold a team-building exercise on the shores of Lake Balaton. Participants numbered around 40–20 from Germany and 20 from Hungary. Most of them were experienced employees; the age group was 30–50.

I was well aware of the differences between the two cultures. Germans are very linear-active – do one thing at a time (thoroughly), are punctual, disciplined and dutiful, and plan well ahead. Hungarians are multi-active – have a relaxed attitude towards time, are imaginative but rather undisciplined, plan well when they are in the mood, but are excellent improvisers when need be. The German communication style is normally straightforward, direct, often blunt; they are wont to criticize if they think something is untoward. Hungarians often feign directness, but they can say one thing one moment and the opposite the next, are adept at covering up their failings, and take pride in their powers of persuasion. One always has to read between the lines.

On the whole the two nationalities do not get along badly. Though belonging to different cultural categories, they have shared alliances in history, resemble each other to some extent physically; the Germans have many qualities which Hungarians would like to possess. Both national groups are highly achievement-oriented. They just get there by different routes.

For the first two days we outlined the different cultural categories, national traits, values and communication styles, expectations of leadership and varying cultural habitats. In the evenings we dined together and socialized over drinks from about 7 to 10pm. Conversation was lively. The Germans drank mainly beer and laid down the law a bit. The Hungarians drank more white wine and agreed with them. When the Germans had gone to bed some Hungarians stayed up and gave me their private opinions. They disagreed with nearly everything the Germans had said but did not wish to oppose them openly – out of politeness and because they had a controlling interest in the enterprise. They exhibited no rancour; their attitude was that, if the Germans wanted to make mistakes, then let them. I pointed out that in all probability the Germans would have welcomed constructive criticism and happily argued the points, but the Hungarians preferred to play it their way. They would follow German instructions as laid down but fail to follow up unpopular directives.

On the third day we gave them an exercise calculated to demonstrate their creativity, competence, ability to cooperate or any other aspirations they had in mind. The task was the following:

By virtue of its acquisitions, Deutsche Telekom was no longer purely a German company. Besides Matáv, it had interests in other European and Asian countries and therefore had everything to gain by denoting itself as an international enterprise, just as the World Bank tries to do to get away from its strongly American image. The participants were asked to build a model with materials that we gave them, to demonstrate the international or cosmopolitan nature of the company. We divided them into three groups – one German, one Hungarian and one German–Hungarian. We gave them an ample supply of paper of all colours, cardboard, matchboxes, balls of string, balls of wool, tennis balls, golf balls, paints, coloured pens and pencils, glue, adhesive tape, a pair of scissors, plastic buckets, empty bottles and various other items which we were able to procure around the shores of Lake Balaton. They had three hours to produce their models.

The Germans started with half an hour of planning and note-taking, assigned various sub-tasks to four or five subgroups, then worked slowly and steadily towards the eventual assembly of their efforts.

The Hungarians had the immediate brainwave of making their model in the form of a boat and started painting, cutting up, gluing and sticking things together after no more than five minutes' discussion. They worked in seven or eight disparate groups with no apparent communication between them.

The German–Hungarian group argued for 20 minutes over the basic idea (using English), started on it half-heartedly, gave up on it after half an hour, made another plan, gave that up too, eventually settled on a third idea which they worked on in two groups – one German and one Hungarian.

The German group finished their model with half an hour to spare and retired to the café for coffee and biscuits. The Hungarian group used up all the three hours but imported coffee into their rooms as they worked. The German–Hungarian group worked feverishly to the last minute, then declared their model was unfinished but they would show it anyway.

We viewed the models consecutively in their separate rooms. The Germans and the instructors judged and commented on the Hungarian model, the Hungarians and the instructors the German model, and everybody (except those who made it) on the binational model.

We looked at the German–Hungarian model first. It occupied the whole floor of the room, had coloured strips of paper leading to all four corners, various original constructions with bottles and boxes crowned with tennis or golf balls, what appeared to be a modern painting and a sign in English 'IT'S YOUR CALL'. A German spokesman described the meaning of the model in English, and nobody understood him. Another German described it in German, and it sounded even more complicated. A Hungarian then interpreted it in Hungarian and found little enthusiasm even among his compatriots. After a polite round of applause, we moved on to the next room to see the Hungarian model.

The company was depicted in the form of a sailing boat. It had a fine square sail (Viking-style), a little cabin, a steering wheel, a rudder, a cockpit, a German captain and a Hungarian first officer. The entire floor was covered in turquoise paper depicting the sea with white-crested waves and the odd floating seagull. Black sharks followed the boat, port, starboard and astern. These represented the competition. Strands of coloured string or wool stretched from the bow of the vessel to various sunny islands and coastlines where happy humans had been painted on cardboard cutouts, all holding telephones (foreign connections). A prominent compass being scrutinized by the captain suggested the ship was 'on course' and would reach its destination. Flags of 10 nations fluttered from the mast. A few rocks showed ahead, representing hazards to be circumvented. The first mate trained his telescope on them. It was a happy, confident model. The spokesman went over the various features just once. The instructors and the Germans all applauded. It was a perfect example of Hungarian creativity and improvisation.

Nobody expected the Germans to take this lying down. They would have their own sleeves packed with goodies. We moved on to the next room to see the German model. It was imposing. It was in the form of a tower – a symbol of power – the international headquarters of a globalized corporation. The cardboard model of the building, 20 storeys high, was hexagonal in shape, and 120 windows looked out on to the world over 360 degrees. On the roof was a penthouse-style control centre. Cables laid at the base of the building fanned out in 18 different directions, each one dedicated to a subsidiary in a foreign land. Flags of 60 nations fluttered from windows and flagpoles. The surrounding ground was transformed into a park with an imposing drive, ample car park and even a helicopter pad. Cardboard cutouts depicted uniformed lackeys helping to park cars and giving directions. A directory board at the exit of the car park listed the different floor functions:

- direction
- administration (three floors)
- building manager
- technical staff
- engineering
- communications centre
- translation department

- accounts
- international training
- international HR
- recreation floor
- VIP suites
- executive accommodation
- restaurant and café
- swimming pool
- kitchen and domestics
- vehicle maintenance
- reception, etc.

The German spokesman outlined the different functions and facilities of the headquarters with no little pride. The audience, particularly the instructors, were quite captivated.

Then one of the listening Hungarians said:

'There's no door.'

The German spokesman smiled forgivingly: 'Sorry, what was that?'

'Where is the door?'

'Door?'

'Door. How do we get into the building?'

Two or three Hungarians walked round the tower to see if there was an entrance at the rear. A couple of Germans followed them.

'There are no doors.'

There was an awkward silence. It was difficult to know what to say; 120 windows had been beautifully painted in, they had knocked up 60 flags in record time, the gardens, drive and car park were beautiful, the human cutouts beamed at the audience.

'It's an impressive model,' I said.

'No door,' said another Hungarian. Some of them have a vindictive streak.

The Hungarian model was awarded the first prize. There were no silver or bronze medals. In the evening after dinner we had a singing competition, which the Germans won easily.

The Hungarians sang out of tune.

TO ROME BY STAG

Once I unwisely drove a Korean friend of mine, as well as our Japanese cook, to Rome in a Triumph Stag. It was a splendid, rather flamboyant, canary-coloured open roadster with a wickedly spluttering muffler which tended to irritate customs officials who were stuck in sedentary jobs on the frontier. They gave us a lot of unwelcome attention, searching our cases and so on, but the real problem was not the car, but the Korean. The son of one of the wealthiest families in Seoul, he was handsome enough, in his prime at 30, but his rugged good looks were those of a domineering gangland mobster. He was one of the kindest of souls, but looked every inch a hired assassin.

We had had some trouble with the French officials, who tried to convince us that Seoul was in North Korea and that Kim was a visa-less commie. Only my atlas settled the question, but by that time our cases had been ransacked and our three lives dissected. I suspected the Italian customs would be worse, and I was right. Kim was grilled at the frontier like O. J. Simpson and accused of much worse than a mere double murder. It appeared he had been sent by Kim Il-sung himself to penetrate the Italian worldwide drug ring while he was in Rome. For an hour my Italian verbs were put to the test. The cook was body-searched, the car underwent the same kind of attention they get in the Ferrari mechanics' pit. The officials in gleaming uniforms paraded up and down like attorneys-general, their oratory was magnificent, their arguments swift and penetrating, but in the end they had to let us go. Even they were not able to move Seoul.

Our three or four days in Rome passed pleasantly, but unfortunately our kind Italian hosts gave me a splendid departing gift: a Peruvian fertility charm in the form of an 8-inch silver fish, bejewelled with rubies, hanging from a chain necklace. It was beautiful, worth a few hundred dollars, but hardly a national treasure.

The border inspector at Ventimiglia – sadly a different frontier from that where we had entered – was very proud of his gold-braided uniform and had considerably greater powers of oratory than his colleagues at our point of entry. He had a field day with North and South Korea, Japanese Yakuza terror and suspicious Englishmen with a yellow Stag and a Finnish driving licence and supposed to be born in Wigan. He attracted a large crowd of passers-by, not to mention a snorting line of French motorists concertina-ing up behind us. When my atlas again won the day, he flung an imperious, bad-tempered arm at the boot and said, 'Open it up!'.

My friends had carefully wrapped the silver charm in intricate layers of packaging and the end result was a sizeable brown cardboard box, sealed with red wax and tied with string.

'*Che cosa é?*' thundered the official. At this point my Italian, which had done reasonably well up to then, suffered a temporary breakdown. A description of my Peruvian fertility offering was now beyond me. Weakly, I uttered the only word that came into my head:

'*Una pesca.*'

'*Una PESCA?*' screamed the customs man incredulously.

'*Si, una pesca.*'

'*APRA!*' (Open it up!)

When we eventually got to the contents, he held up the charm, glistening in the sunlight, for the long line of motorists and admirers to see.

'He calls this a FISH!' he sneered loudly.

We were taken to see the *Commandante*, a gentleman in even more impressive attire, in a sumptuous office a minute's walk away. Kim hung his head like a convicted felon. Tanaka maintained his idiotic fixed grin, and I tried to look like a decent, well-brought-up Englishman, albeit contemplating a lire fine in the billions. The official explained the circumstances to the *Commandante* mentioning Pyongyang and the Italian national heritage at least twice. The *Commandante*, a man with a magnificent head of white hair and an impressive moustache, listened to it all, eyed me coldly and contemplated in silence. What a sense of timing, I thought.

He turned his gaze to the official.

'*ESCA, IDIOTA!*' (Get out, you idiot!), he bellowed. He turned to me and my Asian retinue, and addressed us in impeccable English:

'Gentlemen, I apologize for the behaviour of this imbecile whom I have the misfortune to employ. He is miserably paid, but too much in any case. I hope you enjoy the rest of your holiday. Good afternoon.'

They say that all Italians are great actors, except the ones in the films.

47

A JOKE IN ATLANTIC CITY

At the height of the Cold War, I accompanied a group of German missile engineers to the United States for a conference in Atlantic City, New Jersey. Thirty-nine in number, they were all Bavarian, middle-aged and spoke survival English, although they had a reasonable technical vocabulary relating to their profession and products. They were destined to listen to half a day's presentations given by the Americans, give a couple of their own for half a day and spend a second day discussing contracts. I accompanied them as facilitator – half a dozen of them understood very little English and the group in general had frequent difficulties understanding Americanisms used by the US engineer, such as 'I can't fly by the seat of my pants' or 'it's the only game in town'.

We had a decent flight to New York on Lufthansa with German beer and newspapers and were transferred direct to a five-star hotel in Atlantic City where the Bavarians found the rooms luxurious, the hamburgers reasonable (not McDonald's) and the American beer insipid. They still consumed an impressive amount of it in the hotel lobby where they stayed up till one in the morning and went to bed after a 19-hour day.

They were all on time for breakfast at 7.30am and piled into their private bus for a waterfront drive before the conference began at 11am. I and a few others walked along the beach for

40 minutes, past the Blackpool-type funfair, casinos, pinball shacks, icecream and hamburger stalls, dodgem-car tracks and other amusement halls with flashing lights and blaring music. The resort is handy for New York and Brooklyn weekend- or day-trippers and appealed little to the Bavarians, used to fashionable ski centres and stylish Tirolean architecture. They seemed glad to get into the conference centre and settle down to a day's serious business.

We were shown into a comfortable middle-sized lecture theatre complete with cushioned seats, writing pads, pens and pencils, and bottles of mineral water. The Americans had selected a smiling, personable young man (early thirties) to open the conference and introduce the speakers. Like all Americans acting in this capacity, he had prepared an amusing opening remark, which went as follows:

'Gentlemen, a very warm welcome to the United States and our Fourth Strategic Weapons Conference. I would like to apologize for staging this event in Atlantic City because, as you probably know already, Atlantic City is a very boring place. In fact, it is so boring that when the tide went out last Wednesday night, it didn't come back on Thursday morning.'

Thirty-nine German heads switched left in my direction. As I couldn't think of any suitable expression to assume, I just stayed blank; they all switched back to the speaker. The next hour was all technical, understood little by me, but apparently sufficiently clear to the Bavarian engineers. I knew what was going to happen at the coffee break.

Schulz, the chief engineer, approached me at once. His English was reasonable, but heavily accented.

'Herr Lewis.'

'Yes, Ingenieur Schulz?'

'What did the first speaker mean when he said the tide didn't come back on Thursday morning? In Germany the tide always comes back.'

'Yes, well, it does in America, too.'

'Then why did he say it didn't come back?'

'American humour, Ingenieur Schulz, American humour.'

'*Ach so*, humour!'

He went away to explain to his fellow engineers.

THE AKAKURA SKIER

Akakura is a popular ski resort a couple of hours' drive from Tokyo that draws sizeable crowds during the season, especially at weekends. The scenery is attractive, the slopes long and gentle, suited more to beginners and family skiers rather than to accomplished skiers who seek a challenge. My wife and I belong to the former, more modest category and enjoyed a rare weekend there, though we were somewhat put off by the thronged nature of the main descent. The crowded conditions would be less oppressive if it were not for the presence of a certain type of ski enthusiast known in Japan as a 'kamikaze' skier, who hurtles down the steepest slope he can find in a dead straight line (no slaloms) at breakneck speed, irrespective of whether there is anything in his path – natural obstacle, man or beast. Such characters – obviously enamoured of the sensation of speed – are frequently relatively unskilful skiers, neither wishing nor able to decelerate, should an object or living creature suddenly obstruct their descent. Not surprisingly, collisions are frequent, and people (often the 'obstructers') get hurt.

In order to maximize public access to the slopes (for opportunities for leisure are relatively limited in Japan), the Akakura authorities floodlit the slopes at night from 5 to 11pm. The lights, though adequate, hardly enhanced visibility and collisions occurred with more regularity in the evening. On the

Saturday night, a kamikaze skier of about 25 years of age grazed my shoulder at 50 kilometres per hour and thudded against a plodding individual 10 metres farther down. The 'victim' was flattened but emerged from the incident shaken but unhurt. The speed merchant, however, was less lucky, and after somersaulting three or four times, landed awkwardly in soft snow and was unable to rise.

We approached him, as did many others, and examined the damage. He was lying on his back, legs spread-eagled, with one foot at right angles to his leg. He had broken his left ankle. In typical Japanese fashion, he grinned silently at the ring of onlookers. He tried to get up, but fell back, smiling all the while. He was only 3 metres from me, and I moved forward to help him up; surprisingly I was held back by an older Japanese man next to me. The fallen skier was only 20 metres from the café situated on the slope. Sensibly, he attempted to crawl towards the warmth and shelter it offered. He managed about 5 metres but could not crawl further. He was obviously in pain, though he continued to smile at the dozens of Japanese who were watching him intensely. Again, I was tempted to help him up, but it was evidently not the thing to do. After 10 minutes of feeble progress towards the wooden building, he was clearly not going to make it. Finally, he abandoned the attempt and lay on his back without moving. Another minute passed, then suddenly four Japanese men ran to him, picked him up gently and took him into the café. I had not noticed any sign he gave them, but obviously he had done so, almost imperceptibly.

We struggled to analyse this behaviour, but our further experiences in Japan confirmed our suspicions. A Japanese will not go to help another in trouble unless the latter asks for aid. Such help incurs a debt; the more serious the trouble, the greater the debt. The fallen skier did his utmost to save himself, even with a broken limb. Had he not struggled for a quarter of an hour, he would have suffered enormous loss of face – even more serious than incurring the debt. In the café he not only apologized profusely to everybody within hearing, but he asked for a pencil to scribble down the names and addresses of his four rescuers. In the weeks that followed, they would be the recipients of handsome gifts from the fallen skier. They would of course insist their services deserved no recompense, nevertheless they would accept all gifts, automatically reducing and eventually eliminating the 'debt' in the young man's mind.

A Japanese friend of mine related that he had once snatched a child from the path of an oncoming car, thereby saving its life, but ruining that of the child's father, who, for as long as he lived, tried vainly to repay my friend for his wonderful rescue.

BELIZE

Belize is the kind of country where you would expect cross-cultural situations, though the one we found ourselves in was more unusual than most.

Belize is a small Central American country consisting of a narrow strip of coast adjoining Guatemala, plus an archipelago of several hundred islands (most of them minuscule) in the Bay of Honduras. Formerly the British colony of British Honduras, Belize, which has a mestizo and black, English-speaking population, managed to hang on to precarious independence and escape annexation by neighbouring Guatemala, who was anxious to gobble it up. A small but permanent garrison of British soldiers used to be visible on the streets of Belize City to discourage any Latino incursions.

As we were sailing in the area, we were interested not so much in the mainland strip, colourful as it was, as in the myriad tiny islands of the marine-life-rich archipelago. Some of these islets, 30 kilometres or so off the coast, were not more than 80–100 metres long and 20 or 30 metres wide. It was off one of the very tiniest and most isolated specks of land that we decided to anchor on our first night in the country. Surprisingly, we noted just before darkness fell, that the islet was inhabited. Two small tents were visible just a few yards from the beach and four figures stared out of the dusk at us as we secured our mooring.

At seven next morning two men came over to us in a small boat. They looked Latin American – very dark-skinned – and spoke Spanish. They brought with them five huge lobsters and offered them to us.

'What do they cost?' we asked.

'No money. Just give us some of your food in exchange.'

'What kind of food would you like?'

'*Anything* except fish.'

There were four of them – Mexican fishermen – of an unusual kind. Underemployed in their home country they made the 800-kilometre trip from the Mexican coast of Yucatán to the tiny island where we were now anchored. There they stayed six months a year and fished 12 hours a day. The waters round the island teemed with fish of all kinds, including tuna, dolphins and even sharks. Though they had no other food (the island was a small sandy strip with three palm trees), they supplemented their fish diet with items bartered with yachts people like us, from whom they also got water and, occasionally, beer and other drinks. They were all bearded, wore only trunks and were sunburned from head to toe. They would have seemed sinister, had they not been so friendly (and replete with lobsters).

'But how do you sell your fish?' we asked.

'To the Venezuelans. They come out here in fast launches every two days.'

It was only 130 kilometres to the nearest part of Venezuela and the launches, equipped with two 400cc outboard engines, covered the distance in one hour and a half.

'Do you make a lot of money?' we asked.

'Plenty. We have no competition around here.'

'Isn't life a bit boring?'

'Absolutely. And we are sick of eating fish. But our families live off our earnings for all the year.'

'What do you do during the six months you are in Mexico?'

'Eat meat and *frijoles* and watch TV.'

Ross, our New Zealand skipper, asked them a lot of questions about the marine life in the area. They knew about as much English as he Spanish. Ross was astonished at the variety of fish they landed. They also warned us to take care swimming, as there was a large hammer-head shark currently swimming around the island.

They were going to catch it and invited Ross to come and see it later. When he went to see it around noon, it was there all right, cut up in chunks and filling two huge iron barrels. The Venezuelans were due at three in the afternoon, our friends said. It was OK to swim now, they added.

We invited them on board for dinner after dark. Five nationalities – Mexican, English, American, Finnish and New Zealand – dined well off Finnish pea soup and black bread, Belize lobsters, Honduran potatoes, canned Italian tomatoes, Chilean wine and Colombian coffee. The Mexicans wolfed down everything except the lobsters, which they would not touch.

ABOUT THE AUTHOR

Richard D. Lewis has been active in applied and anthropological linguistics for over 35 years. His work in several fields of communicative studies has involved him in the organization of courses and seminars for many of the world's leading industrial and financial companies.

In 1961 he pioneered the world's first English by Television series, produced by Suomen Television, and subsequently was scriptwriter for the first BBC series, *Walter and Connie*, in 1962. He has lived and worked in several European countries, where his clients included ABB, Allianz, Banco de España, Banque de France, Deutsche Bank, Ericsson, Fiat, Gillette, IBM, Mercedes Benz, Nestle, Nokia, Saab, Volvo and Rolls-Royce.

He also spent five years in Japan, where he was tutor to Empress Michiko and other members of the Japanese Imperial Family. During this period, his services were requested by firms such as Nomura, Mitsubishi, Hitachi, Sanyo, Mitsui and Nippon

Steel. More recently, he has been heavily involved in the inter-cultural field, founding companies in France, Germany, Spain, Italy and Brazil, teaching communication skills in these countries as well as in Finland, Sweden, the United Kingdom and the United States.

Mr Lewis, who speaks 10 European and two Asian languages, is currently chairman of Richard Lewis Communications plc, an international institute of language and cross-cultural training with offices in over a dozen countries. His book *When Cultures Collide* is regarded as the classic work on intercultural issues and was the Spring main selection of the US Book of the Month Club in 1997. Mr Lewis, who is currently cross-cultural consultant to the World Bank, was knighted by President Martti Ahtisaari of Finland in March 1997. In 2009 he was promoted to the rank of Knight Commander of the Order of the Lion of Finland. In 2018 he addressed senior officials of NATO, including the Supreme Allied Commander, in Norfolk, Virginia.

Also available from Richard D. Lewis

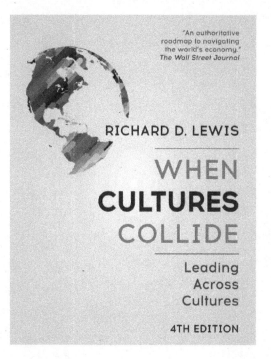

A major new edition of the classic work that revolutionised
the way business is conducted across cultures and
around the globe.

When Cultures Collide provides leaders and managers
with practical strategies to embrace differences and
successfully work across diverse business cultures.

Paperback: 9781473684829
Ebook: 9781473697805

For more information, please visit
www.nicholasbrealey.com

Also available from Richard D. Lewis

Generously illustrated with explanatory diagrams, *When Teams Collide* analyses profiles of 24 different nationalities and suggests how they should be led for best results.

Applying the cultural concepts in the bestselling *When Cultures Collide* specifically to team leadership, this is a wide-ranging and compelling account of how to help international teams work together effectively.

Paperback: 9781904838357
Ebook: 9781904838371

For more information, please visit
www.nicholasbrealey.com

Would you like your people to read this book?

If you would like to discuss how you could bring these ideas to your team, we would love to hear from you. Our titles are available at competitive discounts when purchased in bulk. Bespoke editions featuring corporate logos, customised covers or letters from company directors in the front matter can also be created in line with your special requirements.

We work closely with leading experts and organisations to bring forward-thinking ideas to a global audience. Our books are designed to help you be more successful in work and life.

For further information, or to request a catalogue, please contact:
business@johnmurrays.co.uk

Nicholas Brealey Publishing is an imprint of
John Murray Press.